Enemies
of
AFRICA

Jaiden Baynes

BAYMAR PUBLISHING

Published in Canada by BayMar Publishing 2022

www.baymarpublishing.com

Second Edition

ISBN: 978-1-7780887-5-9 (eBook)
ISBN: 978-1-7780887-4-2 (Paperback)

Contents

Introduction

Black History is important. Black History Month is good. We can stop having Black History Month when people learn Black history with world history. When people learn that Black history is a part of world history.

European history is not only white history. Europe's past is intertwined with Africa's past and the two cannot be separated. North and South America, Asia, Australia, and Europe all intersect with Africa in their pasts. It is less a matter of inserting or adding black history to theirs, and more acknowledging and *no longer* intentionally removing it from our shared world history.

This book is extremely evidence and source-based to attempt to ensure the greatest accuracy possible. However, nobody is perfect, so I would encourage you to check and review sources and know where information is coming from. If any sources provided are known to be less than trustworthy to you, be skeptical unless I was sure to include an additional alternative so that the information can be cross-examined.

As a disclaimer, there will surely be a notable western bias, especially North American bias.

However, the voices of African peoples from the various other nations talked about and discussed in this book should not be diminished or ignored. If they have lived experiences contrary to this book's information, I would strongly suggest you listen to them.

The genius tactician Sun Tzu once said, *"If you know the enemy and know yourself, you need not fear the result of a hundred battles. If you know yourself but not the enemy, for every victory gained you will also suffer a defeat. If you know neither the enemy nor yourself, you will succumb in every battle."*

For as much progress as the black community has made around the world in the African diaspora, there remains the threat that for every one step forward there will be two steps back. Lying in wait for the black people of the world are several cunning enemies that have existed through the ages. Even seemingly defeated foes often rear their ugly heads in modern forms that go unnoticed and unchallenged.

By examining the Enemies of Africa from both yesteryear and today, hopefully, we can all gain further insight into how to counter and finally defeat them in the future.

It is my genuine hope that this book can be the beginning (or continuation) of your journey towards becoming ever more educated. This should not be the be-all and end-all of your educational journey. Attached are many links to sources of articles, documents, and videos to suit various reader preferences for further learning. This book is by no means exhaustive and pursuing any topic written about here can be its own rabbit hole of insightful facts and tidbits.

The goal of this book is to encourage education and learning. To that end, the sources and facts presented here have been curated and fact-checked to the best of my ability. Only sources that seem reliable, are academically accepted or are personally trusted will be included. However, I will not claim to support or endorse the ideological or political positions of *any* sources (especially with content they produce that is unrelated to exactly what is presented in this book). I selected extreme cases where it was obvious that ideology would cloud their integrity however, there are many people that I disagree with on certain things that are nonetheless correct in terms of historical facts so that is all I care about from them.

Speaking of which, aside from ideological differences, their factual integrity is also something I tried to ensure, but nobody is perfect.

Not to sound like I am assigning homework, but I would also urge all readers to look even further into any subject of interest. Separate from any sources provided in this book, always remember to fact-check *everything*.

Generally, the internet is a cesspool of misinformation and fearmongering propaganda (almost deserving to be an Enemy of Africa in and of itself). Familiarizing oneself with the historical method, aspects of journalistic integrity, and other marks of genuine quality are extremely important in this day and age.

However, do not confuse this statement with the frequent weaselly call to 'do your own research,' which is often employed by hacks who lack legitimate evidence themselves.

I would recommend scholarly sources such as Google Scholar and JSTOR. If it says it was written by scientists or historians *make sure it is peer-reviewed*. Without consensus it is bunk. Avoid partisans or those with visible agendas at all costs and always remember to apply a healthy perspective of skepticism before believing anything.

Not to support blacklisting, but it is generally a good idea to keep track of sources that have repeatedly been incorrect. I've made note of sources whose claims should be taken with a grain of salt, many of whom I once trusted.

And please, please, please if you can, do not get emotionally attached to facts you know. If one is married to positions they hold, they run the risk of becoming frothing-at-the-mouth ideologues instead of a truly educated person. Be open to questions and open to alternative ideas. Know why you don't believe something and in turn why you were convinced to believe others. I'd argue it's a virtue to be your own biggest ideological critic, always making sure that *you* know why you believe what you believe and that it is as logical and evidence-based as possible.

A truly wise person is capable of having their mind changed when supplied with evidence. It is better to be right than to be comfortable and to be in the company of the truth rather than 'pleasing illusions.'

Perhaps some sources were simply out of date, or misleadingly titled for a better headline, or straight up ignorantly assumed but the point was it was incorrect. It isn't always necessarily malice but even some facts within this book may not stand the test of time. Researchers call this the 'Half-life of a Fact,' so it is best to occasionally refresh what you know to have the best, most up-to-date knowledge on your interests.

There are varying views on this but to this end, I would encourage being skeptical of sources that do not themselves have sources or citations. Even if the information is a lie, if they are foolish enough to place sources you can debunk them most effectively with their own 'evidence.' That being said, many valuable sources do not cite sources, but you'll never know unless you fact-check them too. Never assume any provider has your best interests at heart but this way you can tell if your source was wrong, or if they themselves fell into a trap of believing a faulty source. But as far down the chain as you can go, be aware of any potential inaccuracies.

As a wise man once said, *"There's too much money in misinformation."*

If the writing seems pretentious at times, I apologize. I learned many new words from reading and researching for this project and was excited to try them out for myself (hopefully they are used correctly). Maybe readers can share in this learning as a form of vocabulary-expanding fun. As a perpetual learner, this first outing in giving back all that has been learned is hopefully a good one.

Please enjoy.

Content Warning, Warning

Warning! There's a content warning on the next page to serve as a warning that warns readers of potentially distressing or upsetting information, images etc. that may be upsetting to them. If this form of consideration for readers is still a thing that people get angry about for some reason *look away*!

Content Warning

This book includes descriptions and images of extremely disturbing topics such as slavery, sexual assault, abuse, and torture. The darker parts of humanity have some unsightly aspects to them. Some potentially distressing sections have warnings ahead of them, but some may be missed so please be aware and read carefully.

Enemies of Africa: Slavery

Portugal whilst a fine country now, principle-wise, the things that the *Kingdom* of Portugal got up to during the 1400s up until the mid-1700s are appalling. While attempting to genocide all the Iberian Jews and Muslims in the lesser-known Portuguese Inquisition, Portugal also discovered lucrative opportunities in Africa.

Portugal began the Transatlantic Slave Trade, a system whereby Africans were stolen from their homelands, sold as chattel slaves, and tortured in some of the most imaginative and horrifying ways humans have thought of.

Of course, the church gave the ok to all this, so it was all above board as long as a sufficient number of them were converted *before* torturing them.

Many other European kingdoms and even the earliest corporations saw the lucrative opportunities of this new trade and began participating as well.

All participants and purveyors of the slave trade are thus… *Enemies of Africa.*

Slavery before the Transcontinental Slave Trade

Let us begin with a brief, simple and necessary definition of a slave. A slave is anyone who exists for any length of time as the property of another and can be compelled to do things for them without compensation (and no, 'room and board' is not compensation).

Slavery is about as old as agricultural sedentary human societies and has served as the basis of much of the ancient world's wealth accumulation and Empire building. It took on different forms in different regions with varying levels of severity and depravity. So, before anyone gets annoying about 'White people didn't invent slavery' no one says that it is. It's an annoying strawman used by oddly defensive racists. But be equally aware that any lies about European Empires being the first to abolish slavery is a lie (abolition was going on from the times of Ancient Persia under King Cyrus the Great). So, let's take a look at those old forms of slavery around the world.

Slavery in Africa

Slave trading in Africa existed long before Europeans showed up. Getting that out of the way before the anti-African racists could have a chance to 'um actually' that fact. African Empires traded slaves among each other with strict regulations on who could be enslaved and the conditions that they were to be kept in. Slavery in Africa was not permanent and the people who existed in slavery (spoils of war, criminals, and debtors) could work the extent of their term and then be set free. Most importantly they could go back to their families and live a normal life after the set time was over. Even better, the children of slaves evaded being labelled slaves from birth. They could also own property and had numerous freedoms and rights that slaves in the Antebellum South could only dream of. Though *much* better than chattel slavery, this was nonetheless a despicable practice of humans owning other humans and is not to be excused. It is estimated that there were 4.5 million slaves (3000-8000 slaves traded a year) within African slave routes.

Slavery in Europe

European feudalism was built on the backs of agricultural labourers called serfs who were forced to do the bidding of their lords. Serfs were not paid for their labour and in fact, had to pay protection fees to the ones who lorded over them instead (often in the form of food or property since money was so hard to come by for them). Serfs technically aren't slaves in the same way that ex-pats technically aren't immigrants. Serfs are property of their lords... like slaves. Serfs are born into that low status and have little to no chance of escape... like slaves. Serfs lived extremely restricted lives as cogs in their owner's labour extraction ... like slaves. Both serfs and slaves could not move or own their own property and had to get their owner's permission to get married. *but* serfs could not be sold by their lord... except when they could (i.e., Russia could sell serfs directly into slavery *and* lords could sell the land and the serfs would be sold part and parcel with it to a new master). Like the ex-pat example, it's a way of diverting negative connotations from the classification. To be clear, serfs had it *way better* than the people most associated with the label slave. 75% of Medieval Europe were serfs. More importantly for our purposes, it should be noted that in many ways, the practice of serfdom in Europe paved the way for the transatlantic slave trade and chattel slavery. Random side note, because I apparently have to say this, *no* the Irish were *not* the first slaves in America.

Slavery in the Middle East

Arabia was well associated with the African slave trade since many of the nation states involved were allies at the time. However African slaves were seen as low-quality slaves compared to Greek, Turkish and Indian slaves. Many Islamic regulations on slavery meant a diminishing number of people who could be enslaved (since chief among the regulations was a ban on enslaving Muslims) and in theory ensured protection from mistreatment. So, the system was very similar to the African slave trade, though slightly harsher given that in Arabia, the children of slaves were often automatically slaves, unless their father was a free man and decided to free them (which became important as many rulers were themselves the children of a female slave/ concubine and the previous ruler).

No matter the race or religion involved, Empire demands the subjugation of others.

The Introduction of Chattel Slavery

So, as it should be clear now, slavery was not a new thing in African kingdoms. How do you think the great African Emperors accumulated such wealth? Slavery like in Rome or Mecca *built* all those Empires. The slavery and subjugation of the poor drove economic growth and were the ways in which leaders could enjoy the fabulous wealth of their resources such as gold. It was rumours and tales of this gold from the great empires like Mali that first caught the attention of Portugal.

Slavery was common in Africa, but European Empires had plans to change things up a bit. Prior forms of slavery were quite common, but the reason the slavery of Africans by European powers was so appalling is that they did not come back.

The notion of a slave not being able to stop being a slave was something the Portuguese and Europeans brought. In central Africa, when slavery started, white people were rumoured to be cannibals because they would keep coming back to take slaves but none of the slaves came back! (Which shockingly might actually be true considering the story of the Arrogante slave ship.)

To be clear, the kind of slavery that Africans thought they were selling their fellow man into was the old practices (still inexcusable but not as bad), but little did they know they had stumbled on a far worse type: 'chattel slavery.'

Chattel Slavery was unlike any form of slavery practiced before. *This* is the cruel and inhumane slavery most of us are familiar with. And this is the slavery that will be discussed in the rest of this book.

To define it here in the words of Dr. Molefi Kete Asante (Asante, 2012)[1]:

"The word 'chattel' is akin to the word 'cattle' and in fact both words share a common origin

in Medieval Latin and Old French. The word capital comes from the same root. Chattel slavery means that one person has total ownership of another. There are two basic forms of chattel, domestic chattel, with menial household duties and productive chattel, working in the fields or mines. Those closest to the enslaver by virtue of space were the domestics and they were usually accorded a higher status in slave society. But to say higher status is not to say much when the idea of chattel slavery was that the human was not a human but a thing. I do not say that the human was dehumanized because I do not hold that such is possible, but what is possible is to reduce another person in your own mind to the level of a cow, dog, cat, or chair. This is the meaning of chattel. As you would not consult your dog, you would not consult a chattel slave. As you would not concern yourself with the comfort of a tool, a plough, or a hammer, you would not concern yourself with an enslaved African's comfort. What is chattel is not human in the mind of the enslaver. A chattel could not have protection under law although there were enough codes to regulate the use of the enslaved."

Source: *Details of Brutal First Slave Voyages Discovered* [2]

The first to capitalize on this strategy of transatlantic chattel slavery was Portugal. Portugal had struck gold with colonies rich in natural resources. But since no one wanted to work in the harsh conditions, they used the age-old tactic of divide and conquer. By intentionally destabilizing foreign relations between African kingdoms and tribes (primarily through introducing guns, as well as a surplus of cows and resources to fight over) they promoted infighting. By perpetuating wars within Africa, Portugal and other European powers could ensure their continued decline in power and a constant supply of prisoners of war.

These prisoners were prime 'workers' for the Empire's newest schemes. Now Portugal could not only pay off the costly Reconquista of the Iberian Peninsula (killing the African Moorish inhabitants of Iberia to establish Portugal in the first place) but keep making money at a horrifying rate.

Slavery was such a lucrative deal that Portugal's fellow kingdoms wanted in on the action and imperialism in Africa began.

As stated before, several Arabic Empires had been buying slaves from Africa before, but even this abhorrent practice was nothing compared to this scale and malicious intent. After all, those slaves were still regarded as some form of human, not chattel.

Meanwhile, European Empires raids stole away so many people that the rulers took notice of the growing ghost towns and desolation left in slavery's wake. In a heartbreaking letter written from the King of Congo to the King of Spain he pleaded with him about the havoc being wrought by the raiding and slaving:

As King Afonso complained in a letter to his Portuguese counterpart in 1526:

Many of our people, for the avid desire which they have for the merchandise and objects of [your] Kingdoms which your people bring here, and so as to satisfy their rampant appetites, steal many of our free and protected people. And it has happened many times that they have stolen nobles and the sons of nobles, and our own relatives, and have taken them to sell to the white men who are in our Kingdoms; and they take them hidden and others go by night, so as not to be discovered. And as soon as they are in the power of these white men they are at once branded with fire and clapped in irons.

Source: *Mbemba Appeal to the King of Portugal* [3]

Raiding up and down the western coast, the Transatlantic slave trade was in full swing.

But today, Portugal has aged out of its Imperialism and most people don't even know about this. Additionally, by no means is Portugal unique in its African imperialism or even the worst offender. They were only picked out for being the practice's originator.

This map shows the volume and direction of the trans-Atlantic slave trade from all African to all American regions

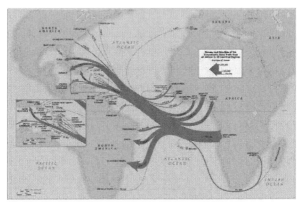

Source: *Slave Voyages* [1]

The Abolitionist movement (people who saw slavery as an evil and fought against it) started almost immediately in opposition to the practice, so people saying that 'people back then didn't know any better isn't an excuse.' Similarly, as far back as 539BC, King Cyrus the Great of Persia declared slavery to be evil and freed all slaves in his Empire, knowing it was the right thing to do long before any modern nation even existed.

The Invention of Racism

To justify the treatment of black people in slavery, black people first had to be defined. This was the origin of modern racism.

Racism created two main categories of people: white people and black people. Obviously, this binary was too crude and nonspecific to be applicable in the real world. So new addendums, classifications and tiers had to be stuck onto it with duct tape in the hopes of continually convincing people that any of it was real.

It all began in the 17th century, during the early days of colonization, wealthy slave owners had a problem. African slaves and poor European settlers were a constant threat since they might ally against the wealthy elites who were exploiting them. To break up this racial solidarity, pushing the idea that the two groups were inherent enemies and not allies was essential.

On top of propaganda being spread, to codify this division certain advantages were given to the new 'white' race with heavy restrictions on the 'black race' to generate resentment between the two 'different groups.' This also ensured that poor whites felt they had more in common with rich whites than poor blacks and no longer supported their former allies who remained enslaved.

So, the battle lines were drawn—white people knew to look down on their black 'lessers' and black people knew that allying with poor white people definitely served no benefit to their emancipation. Divide and conquer at its finest.

But… what exactly defines black and white people?

Black people were easy enough to define— enslaved people from Africa and Africans back home still waiting to be transformed into merchandise.

Whiteness however was a bit more complicated. Colonists came from all over Europe, a continent famous for ethnic groups whom all hated and fought with each other for centuries. To get Europeans to get along, the strategy had to be more conducive to the variable ethnic groups that wanted to be roped in while also leaving room to add any new arrivals from Europe. Therefore, the purity of whiteness was bestowed upon the people who held the most wealth and control, with new inductions into the class being automatic whenever a European ethnicity became economically powerful.

Poor Europeans weren't considered white, and Irish people were despised almost as much as Africans. Germans were seen as 'swarthy,' and some American founders despaired at the thought of their kind entering the country. That was how the original groupings were created. As time went on, the rules changed a bit but mostly remained the same.

Whiteness was and is only defined by what it is not.

It is the ultimate in-group where various racial groups surrender their former cultural identities to join the amalgam against the black race. That was the concept's original purpose and why over time its membership has been so variable.

There is nothing inherent to white people that is either good or bad because the group is imaginary. There are British people, Irish, Italian, German et cetera but there is no 'Whiteland' where white people come from.

At different times, many people who would now be considered white were excluded from that category. Whiteness is seen as the default and so when for example Irish or Italian people were discriminated against, they were done so under the assumption that they *were not* white.

The coalition of ethnic groups that are considered white tends to grow with time as a way of maintaining the solid lead white supremacists feel they must have over the 'other.' Whiteness exists to convince the British, French, Irish, etc. that their individual cultural identities are a part of some mythic collective that has an inherent opposition to the 'other people.'

After all, who doesn't want to be the default of humanity in their own little world?

The only people who can never be white are black people.

Obviously, race mixing complicates all this which was one of the many reasons why purity-obsessed white supremacists of the past (and present) were so against 'miscegenation' aka race mixing.

Biracial people can only be whatever race their non-white parent is or biracial because they have lost their 'white purity' by virtue of being mixed. Since whiteness is based on perceived 'purity' mixed children can never be white. That is why people will say Obama is the first black US president, but next to no one would suggest he continues the proud tradition of white ones.

Nonetheless, the stage was set, and the guilt of slave drivers and owners was thoroughly suppressed for the time being. Now, they could justify doing *anything* to their new 'property.'

Treatment of Slaves

Reminder: All of this treatment was applied to men, women, and children during the Transatlantic slave trade. Useful when talking to anyone who says 'slavery wasn't that bad' in conversation.

During Transport

- Slaves were chained like animals with iron rings around their necks fastened by padlocks for the long journey.
- Anywhere from 250 to 600 slaves would be crammed together under the ship in conditions that pushed many to suicide.

- Overcrowding led to disease, and many died on the way in a dark floating coffin.
- Of 20 million slaves taken into slavery, only half made it to their final prisons.

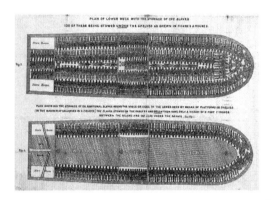

Source: *Liverpool's Slave Trade Legacy | History Today* [5]

If you were a 'good slave'

- Branding irons burned a mark into the slave's bodies that identified them as property.
- Women were frequently raped and forcibly impregnated to save on the price of buying additional slaves and just for general evil and barbaric enjoyment.

- Once the harvest for the year was complete, on some islands such as Haiti that year's batch of slaves were simply left to die (on average only half would survive more than a few years) since it was cheaper to buy replacements than keep them alive until the next harvest.

Source: *Branding of Slaves: Brutal Act Used for Identification Purposes and Severe Punishment | Black Then* [6]

Punishments

- Whipping wasn't very common yet and mostly gained popularity later in the United States' evolution of slavery

- Entire portions of bodies would be seared and burned with an iron, boiling wax, boiling fat, etc.
- A special form of burning was reserved for slaves too ill or exhausted to work or even get up. In that case, they were boiled alive in a vat of scalding sugar
- Mutinies on the ship were once punished by killing the leader and forcing his comrades to cannibalize his internal organs
- Any torture was permitted as long as the slaves remained alive (but as you can imagine, this rule was very lax)

Source: _NPG D12417; 'Barbarities in the West Indias [Indies]'_[7]

Worldwide Abolition

The Abolition of slavery was a long and difficult process that some would argue isn't even over.
The frighteningly recent years and reasons for many
of these abolitions should be surprising.

Reparations

Reparations are a very contentious topic now-
adays which is very confusing because back in the
day, reparations were paid without question... *to the
slave owners*! In Britain, France and the United States
and many others, it was universally agreed upon that
the 'victims' of emancipation should be compensated
but not the victims of slavery. Funny how that works.
All's well that ends well for slave owners, I guess. No
further comment on support or criticism of modern
reparations, I simply hope you consider how quickly
payments were demanded for the slaveholders in the
past (Washington DC paid out reparations of $300 or
$8000 in today's money to slave owners even *before*
abolishing slavery).

Conclusion

When slavery ended in the United States there were 4 million people in bondage. But today there are 38 million to 46 million modern slaves.

Slavery as it existed in the Transatlantic Slave Trade no longer exists. However, do not be fooled, this is much more influenced by the realization that one can simply contract out the slave labour to slave owners overseas rather than take the bad optics of owning the slaves themselves. Slavery is inherent in empires and as long as empires exist anywhere in this world, it doesn't matter the master's race gender, or creed: some form of slavery will persist to serve their greed. Those perpetrators without a doubt are all *Enemies of Africa*.

Enemies of Africa:
The Ku Klux Klan

Source: _El Ku Klux Klan que nació en Nochebuena_ [8]

The Ku Klux Klan (KKK) sucks, we all know it, they are obviously… _Enemies of Africa._

History of the KKK

Source: *Confederate flag: KKK chapter to hold a rally on South Carolina Statehouse grounds - POLITICO* [9]

In the 1860s, the beacon of freedom, America, was polarized by the divisive issue of slavery. In the south, raving white supremacists in the Southern Confederacy of America fought not only for the preservation of but the *expansion* of slavery. In the north, their enemies were slightly less racist Union.

In the South, the Confederate Government's views on the people of Africa were laid bare in the white supremacist bile espoused by Vice President Alexander H. Stephens in his infamous Cornerstone

Speech where he laid out the Confederacy's rationale for seceding from the United States of America

"Its foundations are laid, its cornerstone rests upon the great truth, that the negro is not equal to the white man; that slavery—subordination to the superior race—is his natural and normal condition. This, our new government, is the first, in the history of the world, based upon this great physical, philosophical, and moral truth."

—Vice President Alexander H. Stephens

We won't be going too in-depth on the Confederate States of America here, but yes, they were racist and pro-slavery.

Anyways, the North won the War, and the traitors were utterly destroyed (despite what some believers in the Lost Cause Myth would tell you). However, despite ample opportunities, the victorious Lincolnites took *no* steps to address the racism that still festered in the former Confederate States and reconstruction was a disaster.

The true abolitionists had long opposed slavery, but the weak-willed, spineless politicians were only half-hearted in their attempts at suppressing the sentiments that caused the civil war once it had ended. Almost nothing was done to confront the conditions that led to the Confederacy to begin with and by 1965 as soon as the war was over things got even worse.

After Abraham Lincoln was assassinated, there was almost no opposition to a resurgence in the South. This vengeful racism that was left unchecked coalesced in the form of the **Ku Klux Klan**.

The first Klan was founded in Tennessee on December 24, 1865. James R. Crowe, John C. Lester, Frank O. McCord, J. Calvin Jones, Richard R. Reed, and John B. Kennedy were the names of the original Klansmen. The Klan was founded by these fine Confederate veterans who hated the Yankees (*northerners*) but hated black people even more.

Filled with criminals and sadists, this initial Klan had a goal of suppressing freed African Americans from enjoying the rights they were promised by Abraham Lincoln. The KKK's paramilitary wing (terrorist) was known as the White League and their mission was to intimidate and threaten black people out of voting. Additionally, they engaged in targeted political violence and murdered many innocent black people around the country (mostly in the south).

Fun fact: While researching this, I found out that many White Leaguers later went on to join the early United States National Guard... The more you know.

Source: <u>*Newspaper Illustration Harper's Weekly, October 24, 1874*</u> [10]

The formerly legendary commander 'Unconditional Surrender Grant' who was now President Ulysses S. Grant did little more than give them slaps on the wrist and wag his finger at them for the *constant murdering* going on.

In 1874, the White League attempted to overthrow the State Government of New Orleans in the Battle of Liberty Place. They captured the Statehouse and fought the police and state militia, killing 100 innocents as well as many more men in uniform.

Of course, none of these good old boys were prosecuted and instead had a nifty statue built in their honour which stands to this day with an inscription that reads: *"McEnery and Penn having been elected governor and lieutenant-governor by the white people, were duly installed by this overthrow of carpetbag government, ousting the usurpers, Governor Kellogg (white) and Lieutenant-Governor Antoine (coloured). United States troops took over the state government and reinstated the usurpers, but the national election of November 1876 recognized white supremacy in the South and gave us our state."*

While the White League coordinated violence for the Klan, they also spent their time indiscriminately killing black people around the country for over a century. This was mostly done through lynching. Lynching was the practice of a mob executing people (mostly black) with or without a trial (mostly without a trial) and usually by hanging. Many people were lynched for crimes they didn't commit, and this was simply done to intimidate the black community.

Lynching, a common practice among the KKK was a coordinated form of mob murder between the end of the 1860s and 1968. Though one of the last examples of lynching was in 1981 with the brutal murder of Michael Donald. I'll say it again, a recent case in *1981*.

Even worse, many other suspected lynching occurrences continue to be perpetrated, however, authorities are quick to call them 'suicides' and avoid investigations until public outcry pressures those in power.

The killers or as they called themselves, 'A couple of good old boys' would advertise it as a spectacle (it cannot be understated how many people gleefully participated in these atrocities). Additionally, many newspapers would publish invitations to come to watch the spectacle and talk about it jokingly. Here is a horrific collection of the newspaper headlines that would follow:

Source: EDITOR'S NOTE: No More 'Lynching Logic' to Excuse Brutality Against Black People | Jackson Free Press | Jackson, MS [11]

Source: *MOSH Exhibit On America's History Of Lynching Opens Saturday | WJCT News* and *Jan. 22, 1912: Hamilton, Georgia Lynching - Zinn Education Project* [12]

Source: *"The NAACP's Silent Parade" 1917 Suite | Blackbird v16n2 | #gallery* and *Lest We Forget: The Lynching of Will Brown, Omaha's 1919 Race Riot* [13]

(This newspaper headline was in response to White Supremacists completely flattening the black city of Tulsa. This killed 300 black people, but the two white supremacists also killed take top billing)
Source: <u>Tulsa race massacre of 1921 | Commission, Facts, & Books</u> [14]

The Birth of a Nation Propaganda Film

The KKK was thankfully met with strong opposition early on and as the 19th century turned to the 20th it was on the decline and driven into hiding. Like most features of reconstruction, things were actually best at first before slowly racism crept back in and undid all the hard-fought progress of abolitionists.

A major factor in the Klan's resurgence was a certain propaganda piece known as The Birth of a Nation. Adapted from a book literally called *The Clansman* by Thomas Dixon Jr. the film railed against reconstruction and multiculturalism. It showed the evil of the predatory, degenerate black people being egged on by the pro-reconstruction northern politicians.

It was an excellent recruiting tool that lionized the Klan as superheroes defending white people from the evil blacks and their abolitionist allies.

The movie told a mythologized origin story of the KKK.

The movie revitalized the Klan movement in the 20th century. It was rejuvenated in the states and even spread the blight of the Klan to Canada.

In unrelated news, the Birth of a Nation was the first movie to ever be shown in the White House. President Woodrow Wilson (noted white supremacist and close friend of the original book's author) said of the film, *"It is like writing history with lightning. And my only regret is that it is all so terribly true."* By being screened in the white house, the Klan was able to get an implicit endorsement from the White House.

By 1915, the Klan was *back* and more dangerous than ever before! Local Georgian preacher William Joseph Simmons ran with this second wind of racism and capitalized on Birth of a Nation's huge success. He even hosted a massive cross burning to christen the release of the film in 1915 and declare that the Ku Klux Klan was back.

On opening night, Simmons and fellow Klansmen dressed in the usual white sheets and Confederate army uniforms paraded down Peachtree Street. Role-playing as racist wizards riding hooded horses, firing rifle salutes in front of the theatre. Screenings in cities decided to play along and many even had ushers wearing white sheets to match and show solidarity. The Klan used the film as hot spots to distribute Klan propaganda and seemed to be on track to make a huge comeback.

The Decline of the KKK

For decades the Ku Klux Klan aimed to strike terror in the hearts of African Americans all across the nation of the United States. After a resurgence in the early 20th century, the hooded psychopaths seemed all but invincible. But that was about to change because of: The Battle of Hayes Pond.

James Catfish Cole loved three things, God, his wife, and the Ku Klux Klan! In between his day job as an evangelical minister and touring as a tent evange-list/ Sunday morning radio show host, Catfish was a prolific terrorist as the Grand Dragon of the Ku Klux Klan's North and South Carolina divisions. Though it wasn't actually cool. He spent his nights dawning a Klansman hood and mucking about as a wannabe vigilante spreading his inane and effete ideology of 'white power.'

Source: *Don Cravens/Life Magazine* [15]

Cole harassed minorities across North and South Carolina. Their reign of terror included driving through black neighbourhoods, firing guns wildly and hurling insults and threats at the innocent people in the area. This strategy of scaring the black community and doing everything possible to strike fear in people's hearts had the implicit support from the cops. The police would escort the Klan around to 'keep order' but in reality, sent a message of complicity. This was nothing new of course since the alliance between the police and the Ku Klux Klan was well known and deeply rooted.

With the support of the cops secured and the seemingly endless amount of racism festering back in the 1950s, Cole was able to wreak havoc over his jurisdiction. Raising hate mobs of up to 15,000 to wreak havoc, Cole and the Ku Klux Klan were seemingly invincible.

In the face of this racist harassment and nonstop threats of violence, the black community had to fight back.

Dr. Albert E. Perry was a black doctor in Monroe, North Carolina. As a strong leader in the community and suspected financier of his local chapter of the NAACP the KKK set their sights on him. To begin their twisted attempt at breaking the community, the KKK began sending him constant death threats.

However, little did the Klan know that Dr. Perry's chapter of the NAACP had just received a charter from the NRA of all people to form a local affiliate. This new group called themselves 'The Black Armed Guard' and had a majority of its membership be decorated, WW2 veterans. The Black Armed Guard focused on organizing for self-defence and is relevant for this story, they also provided round-the-clock protection for Dr. Perry from his hooded assailants.

Things came to a head when Cole and his gang of 'good old boys' finally made their move on the 5th of October 1957. The Klan motorcade made its usual rounds to go terrorize the black community and attack

Dr. Perry's house, hollering and firing wildly into the neighbourhood. This time, however, the black community shot back, and the Klan cowards turned tail and ran! After this humiliating defeat, the Klan was banned from Monroe altogether by the city government. The Klan's control was beginning to decline, and they were finally heading towards the dustbin of history.

After fighting the Black Armed Guard and getting thoroughly destroyed, the KKK needed to salvage their reputation with a quick win to show everyone they were not done yet. But after losing to the Black Armed Guard, the KKK began thinking twice before picking a fight with the black community again. The Klan had found that hunting wasn't very fun when their prey also had a gun, so they decided to ease off the black community for a bit.

Despite being best known for their anti-black racism, the KKK also fancied themselves quite the prolific antisemites and haters of Native Americans (they basically hated all people they deemed non-white). For their next attack, they decided to pick a fight with the local native population: the Lumbees. The KKK was honestly stupid enough to be the type to tell Native Americans to go back where they came from, so they obviously were not prepared for what they had signed up for.

James Catfish Cole was as racist to natives as he was to black people, calling them a *"mongrel race,"* he made his hateful intentions clear, *"to put the Indians in their place, to end race mixing."* The Klan got into their usual racist frenzy and preparations were made to hold a cross burning. To be very clear this was intended to intimidate and threaten the natives to scare them as they had done with the black community. As he clearly said, *"There's about 30,000 half-breeds in Robeson County and we are going to have a cross burning and scare them up."*

After several of his usual white supremacist ramblings, Cole and the boys harassed a native Lumbee woman who was rumoured to have had an affair with a white man. They burned a cross outside her home and made it clear that they weren't done harassing the Lumbees.

They obviously had no idea what they were getting themselves into.

In fact, when local progressives and black civil rights groups approached the Lumbee Natives to offer support, they merely replied, *"We've got this."*

Even the cops (again, good pals of the Klan) warned Cole and the boys to ease up on the escalating lest the Lumbees retaliate. But Cole was equal parts racist and stupid, so he continued anyways. He called a Klan rally to be held on January 18, 1958, to 'remind the Lumbee of their place.'

The rally was held and the KKK expected 5000 people to show up. 50 did. Even most of those nutjobs could see the writing on the wall.

Source: *Native America Today* | 🔱 *The Battle of Hayes Pond: How Indian Country Defeated the KKK* [16]

Attacking an entire native community… on their own territory… at night may have been a slight miscalculation. The Klan reached the 'find out' section of the show as 400 brave Native Lumbee fighters thoroughly cleaned their clocks! The Lumbee expelled the foul racists in their show of force as yet again a minority community defended themselves from white supremacy.

It was another humiliating defeat for the Klan and a wake-up call that their time in the sun was ending.

Source: *The Rocky Mount Sunday Telegram, January 19, 1958.* [17]

Here is a political ad showing that the impacts of that victory are still echoed today:

The KKK was horribly embarrassed during an epic thrashing at the battle of Hayes Pond. This marked the beginning of the end for the 'good old boys.'

Source: *File: Battle of Hayes Pond sign. jpg - Wikimedia Commons* [18]

Know Your Klansman

Source: *How white Americans used lynchings to terrorize and control black people | Race | The Guardian* [19]

The bedsheet-wearing cowards got away with too many murders to count. Additionally, no one really seemed to care enough to accurately keep track of the number. We'll never know how many people were killed during those awful times.

The KKK held high amounts of political power with elected representatives all over the country being pledged Klansmen (*especially* in the 1920s). In one instance 30,000 KKK members proudly paraded around the U.S. capital in bedsheets with popular support.

Source: *Decades before the Unite the Right rally, 30,000 white supremacists in Klan robes marched in Washington* and *The History of the KKK in American Politics* [20]

KKK Symbols and Codes

Despite all the evil they accomplished and the dreaded impact they had on African Americans, it cannot be understated how infantile, pathetic, and laughable these buffoons LARPing in bedsheets are. The KKK as an organization has the planning and design of something a child would come up with and it is ridiculous that they have gotten away with so much.

For example, here are the 'levels' these wannabe 'wizards' have:

- **Supreme Grand Wizard**
- **Klaliff** – vice president (from the word bailiff)
- **Klokard** – lecturer (from *Kloran* and *kard*, meaning teacher)
- **Kludd** – chaplain (from Culdee)
- **Kligrapp** – secretary
- **Klabee** – treasurer (supposedly derived from *kaba*, to keep, and *kees*, an Egyptian coin)
- **Kladd** – conductor, in charge of initiating new members
- **Klarogo** – inner guard
- **Klexter** – outer guard
- **Nighthawks** – couriers

Notice that because the genius who started this had the intelligence of a three-year-old, almost everything begins with 'Kl.' The Imperial Khlalif was the second highest position after the infamous post of 'Grand Wizard.' But they couldn't be bothered to come up with a 'kl' name for nighthawks for some reason.

The clubhouse had secret codes you had to know to prove one was a Klansman.

Here are the infantile codes they used

- **A.Y.A.K.** or **Ayak** – "Are you a Klansman?" to be answered by the code below.
- **A.K.I.A.** or **Akia** – "A Klansman I am." These were code words for Klansmen meeting in strange surroundings. They would be inserted into common conversation, for instance, "Does a Mr. Ayak live in this neighbourhood?" to be responded by, "No, but a Mr. Akia does." The password would then be accompanied by a secret handshake or other sign of recognition.
- **K.I.G.Y** or **Kigy** – "Klansman, I greet you."
- **S.A.N.B.O.G.** or **Sanbog** – "Strangers are near, be on guard."
- **Itsub** – "In the sacred unfailing bond," a correspondence sign-off.

- **Sor** – "Sign of recognition."
- **K.L.A.S.P.** – "Klannish loyalty a sacred principle."
- **C.A.B.A.R.K.** – "Constantly Applied by All Real Klansmen."
- **O.R.I.O.N** – "Our Race Is Our Nation."
- **L.O.T.I.E** or **LOTIE** – "Lady of The Invisible Empire." This was one of several names for Klan women's auxiliaries.

The Kalender used to plan meetings was:

- January – **Bloody**
- February – **Gloomy**
- March – **Hideous**
- April – **Fearful**
- May – **Furious**
- June – **Alarming**
- July – **Terrible**
- August – **Horrible**
- September– **Mournful**
- October – **Sorrowful**
- November – **Frightful**
- December – **Appalling**

Modern KKK

After World War II, Hitler and the Nazis were bad optics for white supremacist organizations and changed public perception of racism. Many Klansmen were forced to go underground, but do not be deceived, many of them still walk among us. They might have splintered off into their own new groups such as the Order or the Proud Boys or other organizations of their ilk. This was their strategy of the 20th and 21st centuries. Just a reminder that next to none of these groups are sanctioned as domestic terrorist organizations in the United States at the time of writing. You may identify a KKK member or other white nationalist of their ilk by their calling cards called 'dog whistles.' Dog whistles are secret codes that they know but sound so stupid that normal people don't pay attention.

Dog Whistle Example:

- 1350 or 13/50: Is a White Supremacist Dog Whistle saying that black people make up 13% of the population but commit 50% of crimes. Both these numbers are wrong by the dataset they are misrepresenting.

- (((echo))): a dog whistle used against the KKK's second-most hated enemy; people of Jewish descent ... or Jewish faith? Or people married/distantly related to Jewish people? They never clarify who they're mad at when they say Jew, but ultimately, they're convinced everyone they don't like is Jewish and will put their names in three parentheses to indicate this person or thing is Jewish. For example (((George Soros))) is a common Anti-Semitic calling card.

- 6MWE: A filthy Anti-Semitic acronym which means *"6 Million Weren't Enough."* This not only champions the Holocaust but advocates for a second more complete genocidal project.

- 'Suburbs' and 'urban areas': Usually used by politicians to distinguish between black and white people in America. The dangerous 'urban' people are criminals and a threat to the good old 'suburbs' who need protection. Particularly we have to protect 'suburban women' from dangerous 'urban types' is a favourite among politicians and internet weirdos (a modern form of the KKK's old message). This is a favourite among politicians who want to push forward racist policies without sounding racist.

- 'He was no angel': a dog whistle implying that black people killed by the police deserved to die because they were probably criminals anyways.

- The 14 Words: The 14 words are *"We must secure the existence of our people and a future for white children."* It was the slogan for a white supremacist terrorist organization known as the Order. It has since become a calling card for racists and white supremacists everywhere. They will insist it has no racist meaning even though it does, much like the next dog whistle.

- Western Civilization: A way of saying white without seeming racist. Often used to venerate the perfection and superiority of Western Cultures without sounding like

Nazis talking about the purity of the 'white race.' Even when nonracist people call nations Western without racial intent there is still the unintentional fact that 'western' describes European countries as well as Canada and the US plus Australia and New Zealand (white majority nations, some of whom aren't even in the west on most depictions of the globe). It doesn't make a person racist to use it in all cases, it is just that the definition itself has some history with racist thinking since no African countries, central or south American countries or Mexico get to be western even if they are just as latitudinally west as the actual 'western' nation. Some people use 'global North,' instead, which is geographically more accurate even though Australia and New Zealand still get included somehow. Either way, the 'western' descriptor is clearly a euphemism for something else making it the perfect dog whistle for people intentionally seeking to use exclusionary language. In this book, the term western will be used to refer to those countries however, let it be known that the suspicious definition of the term is not being endorsed even if it is being used.

- Cultural Marxism: An old Anti-Semitic conspiracy theory invented by the literal Nazis that is for some reason still popular among racists. However, they did the bare minimum of changing the original name from Cultural Bolshevism to Cultural Marxism.

- Western Chauvinist: Previous insult that was taken on by racists as a badge of honour. Used by white supremacists to self-identify as white supremacists without calling themselves, white supremacists. As the previous definition states, remember that 'Western' is code for 'White' and a 'Chauvinist' is a person displaying aggressive or exaggerated patriotism... or one could say a Nationalist. Need I say more?

- All Lives Matter: Whenever people try to focus on injustice or problems that minorities face, some are quick to dismiss their protests such as 'Black Lives Matter' with 'All Lives Matter.' Which on the surface makes sense, but I suggest that you question people's motivations when they are so quick to respond with that. Black Lives Matter is not an exclusive statement, and All Lives Matter implies that it is, attempting to hijack the conversation in a way that ironically makes *it* exclusive by refusing to ever address the Black Lives that most people would assume are covered by the All-Lives Matter counterpoint. If the statement All Lives Matter is only evoked to counter and downplay Black Lives Matter, then it implies that the person saying it does not in fact believe so. It's a real 'the lady doth protest too much' situation. By this kind of logic, Dr. Martin Luther King Junior would be racist because of the perversion of his own words against a message he was actually trying to spread. Martin Luther King, Jr. -- I'm Black and Beautiful [21] uh oh! He didn't say all colours are beautiful! This bad faith logic is the go-to of reactionaries who back during MLK's day would counter 'black power' with 'white power' it is always a disruption made to distract rather than actually aid any civil rights proclamations. It may sound fine if you don't think about it, but before repeating 'all lives matter' to counter 'black lives matter' consider the originators of this backlash and why the retort is being employed in the way that it is.

- Reverse Racism: The idea that the racism of minorities against white people is now just as damaging and similarly prevalent as white supremacy is not a new dog whistle. While there are undoubtedly serious problems of racism within the black community (annoyingly both against white people and other minorities) it lacks the systemic power behind it that white supremacist racism has. Being discriminatory against everyone is bad *and* using systems of power to enforce these biases is even worse. Any weird and discriminatory thoughts or acts committed by a black person against a white person are deserving of condemnation, additionally, it must be understood that while this is bad the systemic omnipresence of white supremacy is even worse. It is an extra layer of injustice added on top of any interpersonal racism from white persons to any minority group (white people being racist is not inherently worse, the problem is the real-world consequences that accompany it). It is possible to want to destroy both while admitting that one is much more catastrophically destructive than others. They are equally wrong to do, but the racism of a majority power group against a minority power group will always be deserving of priority given the real-world consequences that systemic power paired with this violence has. Many prefer to say minorities can only be discriminatory but *not* racist. Since that in part helped foster this moral panic about reverse racism, I am hesitant to say that (but this is just my perspective). I don't agree with the idea that minority people can't be racist as an argument of definition; it's a semantics game but I would count being discriminatory as being racist. Instead, I'd differentiate that not just white people but any majority power group in a nation (often ethnic but also frequently religious group) can back up that racism with systemic racism being the manifestation of that racism through systems of power such as law, housing, finances etc. Some people define racism as *only* the systemic racism part but for the purposes of this book, racism is both the discriminatory personal thoughts and actions as well as the systemic actions (so when I mean interpersonal racism it is what such people would mean by discriminatory, this is again mainly just a name game). But just for the people who need this to be said now: minorities should not act discriminatorily toward white people, doing white supremacy but in reverse is infantile and idiotic. Now then, can we work on dismantling the actually dangerous systems of power that kill people?

Conclusion

The modern KKK has rather unimpressive membership numbers (thankfully). However, it is worth putting here to show the origins of modern western White Supremacist movements. The KKK has spawned many other organizations and groups that share its idiotic, racist mindset. Worse yet, its way of thinking has even affected those who would not consider themselves affiliates of such groups. Consider modern manifestations of the above ideas and worldviews and beware the modern spawn of the KKK that still exists as *Enemies of Africa*.

Enemies of Africa:
Colonial Empires

The '*Scramble for Africa*' was the European Empires' sadistic decision to make a game of the complete domination, destruction, and exploitation of the African continent. The untold destruction wrought by this horrifying centuries-long campaign of colonizing makes the participants of such horrors... *Enemies of Africa.*

Colonial Empires are the nations that practiced Imperialism or Colonialism in some form or another in the past or even currently. Throw a dart at a map, and if you hit a nation in the western world, they're probably among the guilty parties.

Imperialism: Imperialism is a policy or ideology of extending the rule over peoples and other countries, for exerting political and economic access, power, and control, often through employing hard power, especially military force, but also soft power.

Colonialism: Colonialism is a practise or policy of control by one people or power over other people or areas, often by establishing colonies and generally with the aim of economic dominance.

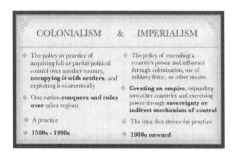

Source: _Difference between Imperialism and Colonialism_ [22]

Source: _THE SCRAMBLE FOR AFRICA Essential Question What was_ [23]

The views of Imperialism and Colonialism have been especially applied to Africa, as seen in this old cartoon of Cecil Rhodes. Rhodes, one of the good old boys, helped the British Empire slice up South Africa and plunder its natural resources. That paired with helping inspire Apartheid bestowed upon old Cecil the undersold title of *Mass Murderer* by Owen Jones. He literally wanted to take over the world and he was only *one* of the many Imperialists of his time. Unsurprisingly his Imperialist tendencies correlated strongly with his white supremacist tendencies as he clearly said himself: *"I contend that we are the first race in the world and that the more of the world we inhabit the better it is for the human race."* Racism and colonialism go hand in hand.

Even worse than Cecil Rhodes was the Iron Chancellor of Germany himself. The worst of Colonialism that continues to have the greatest impact was the partitioning of Africa in the 1800s at the Berlin conference. Basically, the first Chancellor of the newly formed German Empire, Otto von Bismarck, arranged for the great powers of Europe to get together in Berlin and carve Africa up like a turkey (or as this political cartoon from the time puts it: carve it up like a cake).

Source: *THE BERLIN CONFERENCE ON AFRICA 1884-1885 (Vc)* [24]

Everyone got together and argued and bid on sections of Africa like some deranged auction. Here, there were no pretenses about 'civilizing Africa' or 'spreading Christianity.' The Empires were upfront with their desire to cut out large swaths of the continent for military and economic gain.

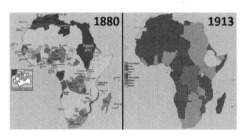

Source: *Mapped: Africa before and after European colonialism* [25]

The lasting impacts of the haphazardly drawn borders created by the imperial powers' colonizing can be directly connected to conflicts and wars ongoing in Africa today. The divide and conquer strategies that worked so effectively in the past were used even more ruthlessly during this time that to this day, people who were once of the same nation or tribe are at each other's throats for completely made-up reasons.

The most well-known result of this would be the Rwandan genocide in **1994,** where the Hutus massacred nearly one million Tutsis. The Hutus and Tutsis are both Rwandans, and the 'division' between them was never racial or even religious. Back in the 1800s, Germany and Belgian simply employed the tried and true divide and conquer strategy of puppeteering the Tutsi into their proxy oppressors to make the Hutus hate them instead of the true colonizer. Germany even went so far as to require that all local chiefs be Tutsis, making the Tutsis feel superior to the Hutu and look down on them while also turning the Tutsis into symbols of colonial rule for the Hutu majority. This completely made-up division was perpetually keeping the two hating each other rather than the ones robbing them blind behind the scenes. Even after Rwanda was no longer a German colony, the hatred between the groups remained until it boiled over into a horrific tragedy.

The Rwandan genocide and other events like it are long-lasting impacts that are still felt today and will likely continue to wreak havoc for centuries into the future.

Colonialism has fallen out of fashion in recent years, but its roots have easily allowed former colonial powers to simply transition into leaning more heavily into Imperialism. Though that isn't to say it's gone completely, since its evolution into neo-colonialism which encompasses cultural imperialism, and the likes have been well documented.

Imperialism and Colonialism are important to talk about relative to slavery. This is because they are what fueled the worst years of the slave trade. To briefly go back into slavery, an often-repeated refutation of the horrors of slavery is that 'the indigenous peoples did it to themselves', which is an easily debunkable argument: _Atlantic Slave Trade: Fallacy of Blacks selling Blacks_[26] And no form of slavery is tolerable, but chattel slavery is by far the worst.

Slavery is one of the few things in history that got worse as time progressed.

In the nations formerly subject to **colonialism**, slavery persists to this day, and there are more slaves in the world today than at any point in human history:

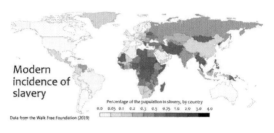

Source: *File: Maps Global Slavery Index 2019.png - Wikimedia Commons* [27]

This map is clearly lowballing the numbers since the United States, infamous for its rampant prison slave labour, is among the highest modern domestic slavers in the world. Land of the Free, am I right?

One of the most overlooked aspects of **colonialism** is the economic exploitation of the subjugated nations. To this day, the world wrings the blood diamonds from Africa using slave labour for international benefit: Blood Diamond Corporations in former colonial powers continue to benefit from instability in the region by knowingly doing business with terrorist groups who use slave labour to extract and sell diamonds to fund their *terrorist activity*.

As it was during the 'scramble for Africa, modern imperialist nations are interested in Africa's vast natural resources: rare metals, gold, plutonium, diamonds, lithium, ivory and of course everyone's favourite, *oil*. Despite the resources being in Africa, almost all the profits of these coveted commodities are taken by the imperial nations and their multinational corporations.

Lest we forget, maintaining an Empire requires constant wars. So, European nations would often conscript members of their colonies to die as pawns in their continued quest for expansion and the colony's own subjugation. Unsurprisingly among the causes of the war, **Imperialism** is one of the key ones: Examples, such as the Treatment of West Indian soldiers in WW1 and African American soldiers in WW1

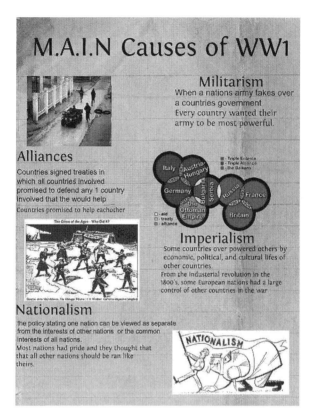

Source: *M.A.I.N. Causes of World War 1* [28]

In the Second World War, even greater numbers of Africans were called upon to fight the Axis. However, after risking life and limb for the war, most non-European involvements were all but completely forgotten by others. Despite being called World War II, many people forget that African soldiers even fought in the war. Once again, the colonies were to be used and then swept under the rug. Many soldiers from African and West Indian colonies were called on to save the Empire, but their achievements were minimized and forgotten. Britain helped win the war, and the idea was that paradoxically, their colonies owed *them* for coming to their rescue rather than the other way around.

Conclusion

Saint Augustine once remarked, *"Empires are nothing but great robberies."* Pirates and Emperors are really the same things, and the sooner people realize this, the sooner the cycle of abuse and suffering can end. Imperialism is bad. From Cecil Rhodes to Otto von Bismarck, those with an eye to subjugate others and inflict suffering upon them for their own benefit are surely, *Enemies of Africa*.

Enemies of Africa: Anti-Africa Bias (Cultural Racism)

These are the people that necessitate this Black history month in the first place. Black History month only needs to exist as long as African history is not taught with world history. People who naturally assume little of Africa may be merely misinformed but, with disturbing frequency, also tend to have a deeply embedded racism. It is not people but this insidious racism that creates... *Enemies of Africa*.

There are the usual people who walk to the other side of the street if they see a person of African descent coming towards them or dog whistle about '13/50' all the time. However, today will be more focused on racism against Africa as being a place of savages and rejection of its respectable past.

People not knowing much about Africa is fine; our public schools couldn't be bothered to teach much about it after all. In general, people don't know much about Chinese or Indian history either, but the cultural consensus does not lead people to automatically assume that they were savages. The idea of Africa being a home of 'dirt people' can easily be traced to the racist archeology of the past, who knew facts but spun things in presentations to deny any respect African societies deserved. The facts have been around for a long time. But only now, without the racism, are people seeing things for what they are.

For starters, people appear to have only recently realized that Africa is not a single country but in fact, a <u>continent</u> (fun fact: the continent with the most genetic diversity in humans is Africa.

Nonetheless, people like to refer to Africa as a single, homogenous unit. Hypocritically, I'm literally doing that *right now*. When talking about Brexit, articles mention it happening in Britain, but they don't say it happened in Europe, or that the Nazis came from Germany, not Europe. And yet, articles mentioning events in Africa will rarely give the country's name unless you're one of the lucky few whom west-

erners care about (Egypt, South Africa, or Nigeria).
Everyone else is usually only mentioned as 'Africa.'

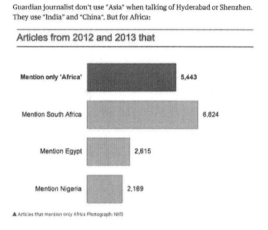

Guardian journalist don't use "Asia" when talking of Hyderabad or Shenzhen.
They use "India" and "China". But for Africa:

Articles from 2012 and 2013 that

Mention only 'Africa' 5,443

Mention South Africa 6,824

Mention Egypt 2,615

Mention Nigeria 2,169

▲ Articles that mention only Africa Photograph: NKD

Source: *Africa Is Not a Country | The Guardian.* [29]

Worse than considering Africa a collective, isn't it
weird how the individual cultures of Africa are treated?

Ever notice how Timbuktu is shorthand for
a place that doesn't exist, meanwhile it is really an
African city in Mali. Or how a Maroon is shorthand
for an unintelligent buffoonish person or moron while
it is an actual group of escaped African slaves from
the Caribbean? Or how Mumbo Jumbo is a name for

foolishness while it is actually part of an African cultural festival? A clear pattern emerges, the repeated diminishing of Africa as a whole.

People who naturally think little Africa can't help but reject the evidence of African civilization with such enlightened arguments as:

mike stone 6 months ago
The Mali empire made some impressive mud castles.

103   REPLY

View 19 replies

Source: *Dumb YouTube comment*

When confronted with actual research, many people immediately dismiss achievements, perpetually refusing to admit any form of advancement of impressiveness coming from the continent. Originally, the argument levied against Africa was that there were no multi-story buildings. When basic research could prove otherwise, the reaction was a typical motte and bailey deflection *(when they refuse to admit they were wrong by just moving the goal post)*. Strangely, it is as if they're only looking for reasons to justify their predisposed hatred or dismissal of the land they were conditioned to look down on.

Calling the massive palaces 'mud castles' betrays their cultivated bias. Our modern-day brick is mostly made of sand and clay. But some people refer to this 14th-century African castle, also made of sand and clay, as a 'mud castle' to diminish and mock its impressiveness. Their feeling of superiority over anything African is loud and clear.

Source: *African "Mud" Castles* [30]

Calling that a mud castle is comparable to being racist against the British and downplaying their architecture by saying, *"The British Empire built impressive stone huts."*

Source: *Royal Residences | Windsor Castle - Royal.UK* [31]

Richard Nicklin Hall is a perfect example of this nonsense even at the academic level. When the British discovered the magnificent buildings in Zimbabwe, they wanted to get experts to study this fascinating monument. This monument was a gorgeous stone wall similar in integrity to the castles of Europe. This site was completed with a drainage system that functions to this day and a solid outer brick wall on par with Europe's contemporary (actual) motte and bailey castles. The Zimbabwe city was built sometime between the 11th and 14th centuries, without needing mortar.

The archeologists were astounded and, of course, initially attributed it to a fictional tribe of Europeans who supposedly had settled the savage lands and done it themselves (or demons or whatever). They eventually settled on a crackpot theory that it was the palace of the Queen of Sheba mentioned in the Bible; hence it wasn't African. Ironically, the Queen of Sheba was from either modern-day Ethiopia, Somalia, or Eritrea. So… it would still be African.

Source: *Great Zimbabwe Ruins* [32]

While they refused to accept the idea that Africans built it (*despite literally every piece of evidence pointing to that conclusion*), Richard Hall, the journalist there to chronicle their discoveries, dealt with this challenge to his biases *very* differently.

Hall's one job was to watch the site so it could be studied and recorded; that was his one job. However, by the time the archeologists returned to study it, **Hall** and his men were already halfway through demolishing the site to try and completely destroy it. When asked why he would destroy such a marvel of ancient architecture, he replied.

"[My] recent and timely preservation work... removing the filth and decadence of [redacted] occupation." - Richard Nicklin Hall

Source: *Nick Fuentes and the African Wheel* [33]

Take a guess what the word [redacted] is.

This violent rejection of learning shows the cycle of rejecting African achievements that plagued the archeological community in the past. They assumed Africa was unremarkable and savage, so, when they found evidence to the contrary, they destroyed, obfuscated, or misattributed said evidence. Thus, the next generation would repeat this cycle, over and over.

Now, in modern times, racists can confidently say such nonsense as the idea that Africa didn't even invent written language, multi-storied buildings, or the wheel. There's nothing wrong with not knowing, but an insistence on confidently saying untrue things about Africa for the purposes of racism is disgusting.

Similarly, in modernity, there is a strange insistence among conspiracy theorists that aliens instead of Africans constructed all of the impressive monuments in Africa. This is most prevalent and annoyingly seen with the pyramids.

However, these 'ancient aliens' conspiracy theories and 'ancient Atlanteans' conspiracy theories tend to be ideological descendants of 'ancient Aryans' conspiracy theories. Hate to invoke Godwin's law but the insistence that Africans and other 'lesser races' could not do these things by themselves was a common Nazi talking point.

This kind of thinking causes many people to use the 'slaves were better off as slaves than back in Africa' myth. Best put by beloved cultural icon, Robert E. Lee:

THE BLACKS ARE IMMEASURABLY
BETTER OFF HERE THAN IN AFRICA, MORALLY,
SOCIALLY & PHYSICALLY. THE PAINFUL DISCIPLINE
THEY ARE UNDERGOING, IS NECESSARY FOR
THEIR INSTRUCTION AS A RACE, & I HOPE WILL
PREPARE & LEAD THEM TO BETTER THINGS.
HOW LONG THEIR SUBJUGATION MAY BE NECESSARY
IS KNOWN & ORDERED BY A WISE & MERCIFUL PROVIDENCE.
- ROBERT E LEE

Source: _Robert E. Lee_. [34]

Aw, isn't that sweet? He thinks the poor savage Africans need to be 'whipped into shape' for their own good (literally). This paternalistic and condescending attitude towards Africa is communicated by most who assume Africa was some horrible backwards place where people lived in bushes and ate mud.

These continuous micro-aggressions are nowhere near as bad as slavery or colonialism but show the continued effect those past forms of racism have on modern times. This shows western culture's strange relationship with Africa (it's not an individual problem, we all do it from time to time).

Honestly, coming into this project, I severely underestimated several African nations and assumed less of them before reading further. Even nonracist people think very little of Africa, so it is important to be educated and to educate others to stop this from continuing.

Keep an eye out for strange anti-African sentiment and reflect on its presence being so ingrained in the world around us.

Conclusion

It is hopefully an uncontroversial statement to say that there is a general ignorance of the history and culture of Africa. The anti-African bias ultimately stems from this ignorance and an inability to accept Africa as an equal to the civilizations that the west has deemed to be worth talking about. Education on such things is sorely lacking and so perhaps it is unfair to point fingers at the general public for this. Those who do not know can come to admittedly racist conclusions, assuming that since their underfunded, racist education system says nothing of Africa then there must not be anything there worth talking about. To the readers from the continent of Africa and Africa buffs, I beg your patience with them, the buck does not stop there. The buck stops with the designers of said underfunded, racist education systems with western supremacy and African ignorance. Those who don't know, don't care or don't care to know when communicating the history of over 2 billion people to the masses. This modern conundrum did not occur by accident or sans any revisionism or machinating. Any ignorance of Africa and subsequent pride-induced downplaying of Africa now that more knowledge is being spread falls at the feet of the likes of Richard Niklin Hall. May the long line of pseudo-intellectuals, journalists and others who bare their racial agenda against the dark continent end now. Because every one of them who occupies that long line of frauds are, *Enemies of Africa.*

Enemies of Africa: 'Scientific' Racism

Biology, anthropology, and genealogy are vital and essential fields of scientific study and can provide essential insight into the world around us. However, the predecessors of these fields are not so helpful. Instead, they are unbelievably detrimental, especially to minorities. Practitioners of early studies of human-kind almost exclusively did so with a racist motive in mind, hoping to prove the genetic inferiority of the 'lesser races.' Because of this, these despicable pseudoscientific practices and their quack inventors are undeniably... *Enemies of Africa*.

Pseudoscience: statements, beliefs, or practices that claim to be both scientific and factual but are incompatible with the scientific method.

With that completely unrelated definition out of the way, what could be so harmful about the innocent study, categorization, and stratification of the five (5) races: Caucasoids, Mongoloids, Australoid, Capoid and Negroid races? Let's find out.

Source: _The five races of Mankind according to this German poster, 1911 - Rare Historical Photos_ [35]

Well, first of all, to get it out of the way, these quacks were not scientists. Science and the word 'theory' have been tainted by kooks, crackpots, and propagandists who take advantage of society's general ignorance about science. Because of this, people fall for 'conspiracy theories' and the like, which are a perverse bastardization of the word 'Theory.' The term

'Theory' in science is only reserved for the most well-proven and irrefutable observations and ideas (*it is borderline offensive to use the word so flippantly and casually*). In science, things are not a *theory* until they have been extensively peer-reviewed and scrutinized.

Modern science is relatively new, only coming into being in the 17th century thanks to Francis Bacon's genius. It follows rigorous processes outlined by the scientific method and anything not adhering to this process *is not science*. No matter how many statements or award-winning books come out, if it isn't peer-reviewed, then it is not science.

For the record, anything invented before the advent of the scientific method *is not science* until it passes the scientific method and is replicated by others for consistency in the process of peer review. If we accepted it as fact before the method, it must still pass the scientific method's scrutiny to be considered today. Anything that does not hold up is discarded with extreme prejudice. In the scientific community, there is a zero-tolerance policy toward pseudoscience, and it would be greatly beneficial if this stance were adopted by the general public as well.

The Scientific Method

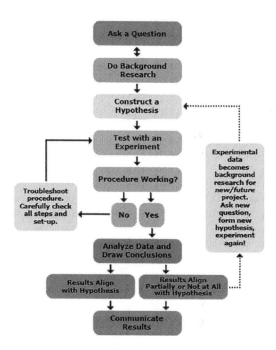

Source: *Steps of the Scientific Method* [36]

This is the process by which real
science is carried out.

Phrenology

Succinctly described by the Simpsons, Phrenology is, *"Quackery that was dismissed over 160 years ago."*

Phrenology is the study of personality traits, talents, and mental abilities due to skull curvature and other features of the head. This is completely made up. However, despite this, it was widely taught and practiced until the 1960s.

Extensive diagrams were pulled out of nowhere to explain that the average head and face shapes of people from around the world were not responses to external factors such as temperature, precipitation, and sunlight (as we know them to be today). Instead, phrenology argues that differences in skull shapes are because of racial superiority or inferiority.

Not only did phrenology consider the skull and parts of the brain but also nose, ear, and brow shapes. Phrenology assumed that the shapes and sizes *of these features could tell someone everything they needed to know about a person and even what their job should be.*

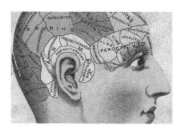

Source: *Walt Whitman, America's Phrenologist - JSTOR Daily* [37]

Source: *writing de jure » History of Criminology* [38]

Phrenology is deeply engraved in western culture to this day. For anyone familiar with the terms 'highbrow' and 'low-brow' as adjectives describing a person's intelligence, these are terms from phrenology. Not just brain size, but a person's hairline was important too.

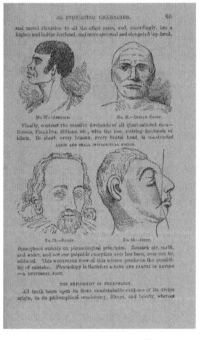

Source: *Phrenology* [32]

Not surprisingly, colonial powers saw fit to assign their human property (Africans) consistently low levels on the perverse tier list of humanity that emerged from phrenology. Using this absurd practice, phrenologists contradictorily concluded that Africans were inherently aggressive, energetic, and impulsive, but they were also passive, lazy, and incapable of making decisions independently. Here are some ridiculous pictures shared by phrenologists and touted as 'science' to justify existing racist stereotypes (play a fun game and try to spot the hidden racism!).

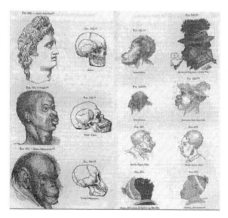

Source: _Phrenology and "Scientific Racism" in the 19th Century | Real Archaeology_ [40]

Of course, in the end, *phrenology* was just an excuse for racism. For starters, non-white races were considered sub-humans as negroes, Indians etc. and the shapes of their heads were used as justifications for perceived stereotypes.

MALE SKULL.   FEMALE SKULL.   INDIAN SKULL.   NEGRO SKULL.

Wells' representation of four skulls

Source: <u>*No. 2148 American Phrenology*</u> [41]

This nonsense was used by racists to justify their mistreatment of minorities and to assert their own superiority. Wealthy European people decided arbitrarily that their skull shapes were the general ideal and that others had to work hard as their servants (and slaves) in the hopes of ever attaining the 'right' skull shape.

Thankfully, phrenology has mostly fallen out of fashion after WW2.

Additionally, phrenological institutes such as the British Phrenological Society didn't get around to being disbanded until disturbingly recently (1967).

Phrenology is still around somewhat, especially in circles of racists seeking to use it to justify racism (as its founders intended).

"*Why would racial differences be only from the neck down?*" is a phrase often used by racist and modern phrenologists. This is a logical fallacy used as a trojan horse by racists to insist that if black people have different skin tones, then the brain must be different as well. I'm afraid that's not right.

Long story short, the massive chunk of DNA that codes the brain is *much* more complicated and difficult to change (*hanging out in the desert for a few generations may change your skin tone but will have zero effect on the brain*).

People who insist Africans have smaller brains and so are less intelligent are also dumb. Brain size doesn't matter as much as neuron connections. Even neuron connections are not the end-all and be-all that explains intelligence. There are many animals with more neuron connections than humans, and they're nowhere near as intelligent.

It is almost as though human intelligence is far too complicated to be measured by such archaic means. Besides, wouldn't phrenology also imply that shorter people are dumber and taller people are smarter? Would a tall black person be smarter than a short white person? Or does the size of other organs affect human intelligence as well? None of it makes any sense.

Another way in which phrenology has stuck around in modern thinking is strange pseudoscientific beliefs about 'left-brain' and 'right-brained' people. This isn't real.

This pseudoscience nonsense seems benign, but in fact, can always be connected to the misfortunes and tragedies that befall Africans and any other minorities. It has been used to justify genocide, slavery and the continued subjugation that continues to this day. Pseudoscience is just plain dumb.

Eugenics

"Eugenics is the practise or advocacy of improving the human species by selectively mating people

with specific desirable hereditary traits. It aims to reduce human suffering by 'breeding out' disease, disabilities, and so-called undesirable characteristics from the human population."

Extending from phrenology, Eugenics was *huge* in the 20th century. Before Hitler made it the main focus of Nazi Germany's twisted domestic and foreign policy, it was a favourite topic among eugenics societies. Eugenic societies were groups of weirdos with too much time on their hands who got together and discussed why genocide was just swell. Prominent members of these groups included (*and I do wish I was making this up*): George Bernard Shaw, Helen Keller, Alexander Graham Bell, Theodore Roosevelt, Winston Churchill, and John Harvey Kellog.

The goal of **Eugenics** is the sterilization, marginalization, and eventual genocide of all 'lesser' peoples for the sake of superior peoples (sound familiar?). More than 60,000 people have been sterilized in the United States alone, and not surprisingly, most of them were African American.

Source: *The Bell Curve* [42]

After the holocaust, eugenics quickly lost public support, but like everything else mentioned here still lurks in the shadows among weirdos, racists, and ignorant people.

Eugenics was, of course, bolstered by and intrinsically connected to…

IQ

Now don't get mad… but IQ isn't real. Sorry, it's not. If IQ was real and intelligence could be mathematically and quantitatively represented by taking a test with no biases whatsoever, feel free to solve this 1st grader question.

抜けている形を選択する。
二、四、六、＿
A: 九
B: 七
C: 十
D: 八

Source: *The Bell Curve* [43]

Nonetheless, IQ back in the day was *huge*. At its height, IQ tests were required for immigration into certain nations (like the United States in the 1920s).

Even today, it is the tried-and-true method for racists to justify feelings of superiority over others. People who obsess over this stuff call themselves 'race realists', which is a polite way of self-identifying as a Nazi (complete with antisemitism, eugenics and all the despicable things of the like). Race realism is built on an obsession with race and IQ to stratify the races into a hierarchy.

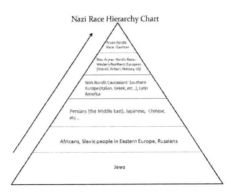

Source: *The Social Meaning of Race & Ethnicity - ppt download* [44]

Hey! How did that completely unrelated image get there?

These backwards ideas persist in modern times and, despite people insisting otherwise, are disturbingly common in the western world with prominent websites, YouTube channels, podcasts and magazines spreading their ideas. Its unwelcome return has had serious consequences.

Race realism is an insidious idea being widely spread online and to youth as a talking point to justify a white ethnostate (a nation only for white people where all others are … removed).

In an infamous example of this old-fashioned view sticking around, James Watson, a scientist who helped discover the double-helix structure of DNA, had many of his titles and honours revoked after he expressed views saying racist things about IQ.

He rambled that he was, *"inherently gloomy about the prospect of Africa,"* because *"all our social policies are based on the fact that their intelligence is the same as ours—where all the testing says not really."* And to sum up his feelings rather concisely, he said that while it would be great if all races were equal, *"People who have to deal with black employees find this is not true."*

This brain poison is widespread and has to be stopped. Prepare for an attempt at extensive debunking!

Levine and Marks 1928 IQ classification[44]

IQ Range ("ratio IQ")	IQ Classification
175 or above	Precocious
150–174	Very superior
125–149	Superior
115–124	Very bright
105–114	Bright
95–104	Average
85–94	Dull
75–84	Borderline
50–74	Morons
25–49	Imbeciles
0–24	Idiots

Source: *IQ classification - Wikipedia* [45]

Not scientific, but as a personal example to fully grasp the pseudoscientific nature of IQ, I took 3 different IQ tests within a few days and ended up in 3 widely separated levels, with the greatest discrepancies being a difference of more than 50 IQ points.

The greatest perpetrator of the IQ myth and IQ's relation to race is a book called 'The Bell Curve.' This book was written by famed white supremacists Charles Murray and Richard J. Herrnstein. Only one is a psychologist, and neither is properly peer-reviewed. That's a good sign.

Charles Murray, chief among the two, has an extremely shady (and racist) past as discussed here: Charles Murray

The full quote basically does all my work for me, so here are the relevant sections:

"The book shows that, on average, blacks score about 15 points lower than whites on intelligence tests, a point that was widely known and has not been in dispute. Mr. Murray and I (and many, many others) differ on the reasons for the disparity. I would argue that a group that was enslaved until little more than a century ago; that has long been subjected to the most brutal, often murderous, oppression; that

*has been deprived of competent, sympathetic politi-
cal representation; that has most often had to live in
the hideous physical conditions that are the hallmark
of abject poverty; that has tried its best to survive
with little or no prenatal care, and with inadequate
health care and nutrition; that has been segregated
and ghettoized in communities that were then red-
lined by banks and insurance companies and otherwise shunned by business and industry; that has been
systematically frozen out of the job market; that has in
large measure been deliberately deprived of a reason-
ably decent education; that has been forced to cope
with the humiliation of being treated always as infe-
rior, even by imbeciles -- I would argue that these are
factors that just might contribute to a certain amount
of social pathology and to a slippage in intelligence
test scores.*

*Mr. Murray says no. His book strongly suggests
that the disparity is inherent, genetic, and there is little to be done about it ....*

*The last time I checked, both the Protestants and
the Catholics in Northern Ireland were white. And yet
the Catholics, with their legacy of discrimination,
grade out about 15 points lower on I.Q. tests..."*

Even funnier, IQ is further debunked by the Flynn Effect, a psychological phenomenon whereby the average IQ of people has consistently risen by 15 points in the past century, and so the average IQ score must continuously be readjusted back to 100 to compensate. This means that black people today are on average smarter than white people in the 50s. Or is it just that after desegregation, black people's living conditions have considerably improved, allowing for better education? Who can say?

The Bell Curve is extremely unscientific, and yet it is widely circulated around to bolster claims of African inferiority. Mentioning the Bell Curve should be met with equal skepticism as any other dog whistle.

Conclusion

Racism is stupid. Racists know racism is stupid and based on emotion, not logic. Racism's goal is to create the 'other' and to make them an object of fear and hate for whatever majority power group vomited it forth. It is not sensible; it is not scientific, and it is not true. Racism's bastardizing of science predicates solely on their hatred of science. How many people who support racist pseudoscience also endorse the scientific method? And how many submit and accept the scientific model of peer review? Racism detests science as much as it detests facts. That is why racism as conducted through the racists that this vile symbiote possesses opposes scientific education, but instead, a sheep-like acceptance of their findings is encouraged. *This* is science in the minds of the useful idiots duped by racism. There is an almost contemptuous condescension from the leaders of 'scientific racism' that know in their hearts, if they ever had any at all, that no one is going to fact-check on them. They lie, they say they are scientists and then argue against showing sources, argue against obvious debunking of sources if any are provided and argue against science and reality. Racism is stupid and may the word science never be forced to exist next to it *ever again*. Remember that racists will come up with any excuse for their racism. Making up fantastical and absurd metrics to place races in a hierarchy or obsessing with skull shapes or made-up numbers are just a few. But they are equally absurd and unscientific. Pay this vile tendril of racism no mind and for the love of all that is Holy, *do not ever* let it come back into fashion. These pseudoscientific hacks and those numb-skulled idiots who try to revive their quackery are all, *Enemies of Africa.*

Enemies of Africa:
Divide and Conquer

Much of Africa's progress has been impeded by hostile forces seeking to turn brother against brother and weaken the continent as a whole. This process has been unfortunately effective and so passed from one foe to the next as a winning strategy to oppress the dark continent. The perpetrators of this vile technique and all those who aid them in it are all clearly... *Enemies of Africa.*

As a review of sorts, let's now examine a few examples of invading or colonizing powers encouraging and strategically facilitating infighting within Africa as a form of Divide and Conquer strategy.

- Hannibal Barca's African mercenaries were bribed and recruited by the Romans to fight against him and the African republic of Carthage

- Nzinga actually fell prey to this trap and helped the colonizers seek and destroy her fellow Africans over tribal squabbles (though she notably gave the colonial powers a taste of their own medicine in that regard as well)
- The Zulus fell prey to economic disruptions caused by settlers and began warring over resources with fellow tribes over the economic pressures
- Cetshwayo's brother became a stooge for a failed British-sponsored coup d'état attempt
- Sambo aided his owner in the oppression of his fellow slaves

And so on and so forth…

The strategy works. And frighteningly continues to work.

Even before being put to work on Africa, the Empires of the past worked out its frightening effectiveness.

In Europe for example, traitor to the Greeks Alcibiades of Athens recommended that the Persians let their ancient enemies the Greeks fight amongst themselves until their own divisions destroyed the fragile alliance that had saved them from the Persians in the past. '*The cheapest plan was to let the Hellenes wear each other out, at a small share of the expense and without risk to himself.*' The war he dreamed of was realized and in short order, the fractured city states imploded into embarrassing and disastrous declines (though ironically the Empire to capitalize on this and conquer them was Alexander the Great's Macedonia and not Persia).

In Asia, European powers waited for Japan's industrialized Empire to smash the old and waning Chinese Empire so that they could swoop in and carve it up for themselves.

In Africa, by now everyone knows the story. But the divisions of the past have yet to heal. Violent religious and political factionalism that lingers from the days of being puppet states for rival Empires maintains animosity and a sense of incompatibility between fellow African states. Even within the borders drawn by European partitioning, the tension between ethnic groups and other divisions remains a problem.

A famous example is the Zulu and Xhosa divide in South Africa. Both were equally oppressed by the Dutch and British Empires throughout their histories. But each is also convinced it is the other's fault for their oppression. As Trevor Noah said in his book *Born a Crime,* "*The genius of apartheid was convincing people who were the overwhelming majority to turn on each other. Apart hate is what it was. You separate people into groups and make them hate one another so you can run them all.*"

The divide and conquer mindset were so effective that it arguably remains to this day!

Recently, there have been pushes to unite Africa into a union similar to the European Union. But once again, Africa's colonial past rears its ugly head.

Despite all that, intergovernmental organizations like the African Union (formerly the Organization of African Unity) are trying to resist and help African nations unite and advocate for their collective, integrated interests.

One of their most ambitious plans is called Agenda 2063 which they describe as:

"Agenda 2063 is the blueprint and master plan for transforming Africa into the global powerhouse of the future. It is the strategic framework for delivering on Africa's goal for inclusive and sustainable development and is a concrete manifestation of the Pan-African drive for unity, self-determination, freedom, progress, and collective prosperity pursued under Pan-Africanism and African Renaissance."

All African nations are currently members of the African Union and have ambitious plans to help Africa recover from past and current foreign meddling. Despite being around a long time (since 1963, they haven't achieved all their goals). This won't completely fix the problem, but it is a step in the right direction.

So, what's the lesson here? Well, history is to be learned to avoid repeating the same mistakes. And thankfully a natural defence against these tactics has begun developing, especially and most effectively around the Civil Rights Movement in the United States of America.

Martin Luther King Jr. and Malcolm X criticized and challenged each other, but not destructively or as adversaries. There was much to fight about but their contrast was simply a diversity of tactics

They were not divided by methods or religion or politics but instead, they were united by goals.

Source: *Martin Luther King Jr. and Malcolm X Only Met Once - Biography* [46]

Conclusion

African Americans or Canadians or Britons or whatever may feel pressured to look down on Africans from the mother continent. But divide and conquer is not only an issue within the worldwide black community. Letting African people be turned against any other minority group is to fall prey to divide and conquer. Never kick down. But also remember that letting African people be taken in by racial hatred against potential white allies is also to fall prey to divide and conquer. Minorities hating other minorities is crazy and should never be fallen for. We wrestle not with peoples and races but with hierarchies that pit human beings against each other, with systems of power that suppress and oppress and those in high places of any race, gender or creed that orchestrate and perpetrate such tactics as divide and conquer. *Those* are among the truest *Enemies of Africa*!

Enemies of Africa: Neocolonialism and Resource Exploitation

"There are starving children in Africa," is a form of guilt-tripping that many of us are familiar with in the west. It is one of the best examples of the omnipresent perception of Africa being mentioned. But no one ever stops to think about it. Why is Africa so relatively poor?

If you're a racist, the answer is obvious, *"Because of all the black people."* In fact, even if you aren't a racist, this is typically the response people give or hear.

However, rather than a race-based answer, a political and economic inquiry can yield far more accurate and useful results. A lot of this comes down to how these African countries were established in the first place. Sadly, a lot of the past ills that befell the continent continue in some form today. Everything that's old is new again! Colonialism is now neocolonialism, and the exploitation of the past is kept alive by foreign interests.

This racket requires a lot of key players. The IMF, multinational corporations, and even corrupt politicians in those African countries themselves. These government officials who sell their people out for a quick buck are typical Sambos.

Their scheming and plotting to exploit the many resources of the dark continent make them … *Enemies of Africa.*

The IMF, World Bank and Neocolonialism

After WW2, Britain and France were broke and exhausted. Subsequently, France fumbled away many of their colonies in exchange for a last-ditch effort to keep their favourite Algeria. Ultimately, they did not. France didn't give up Algeria. The Algerians forced them out after 130 years of brutal oppression. The

British Empire on the other hand couldn't afford the liabilities with their exhausted Empire and so let their colonies go not out of the goodness of their heart, but more to avoid them becoming a problem. France's colonies like Algeria and Vietnam were rebelling and Britain figured it was better to cut theirs loose themselves rather than to lose an embarrassing war trying to maintain control and then fail. Kind of like England did with Kenya anyways…

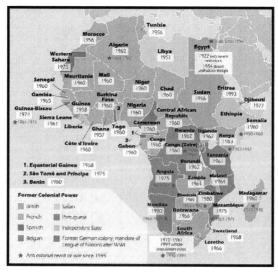

Source: *Objective 11- Antharya - Chapter 37* [47]

So maybe, even saying that they 'gave up' their colonies would be inaccurate. Most will be surprised at how late many of these infant nations were 'given up' by the overbearing parent Empires.

Either way, 'peacefully' or violently, this sudden change was not the smoothest transition for many African countries. The complete extraction of stable government and wealth while leaving no infrastructure or stable power in Africa de-stabilized the nations in their early years. They *had* good governments in the past, but the colonizers couldn't be bothered to leave stable new ones after destroying and replacing the old.

No need to worry though. While direct colonization was so 1800s, the western powers still intended to make client states of Africa yet using the next best thing, the Private Sector!

In the old days, companies would just move in and run the place. Through policies like that, Empires can maintain distant control of former colonies to this day.

Additionally, a notorious perpetrator in this ransacking of Africa is of course the De Beers diamond company. Now it may come as a surprise, but this 3.4-billion-dollar conglomerate was founded by our old friend Cecil Rhodes. Y'know… that guy: the Ultimate Imperialist:

Cecil Rhodes

- British imperialist who made huge profits from Africa's natural resources
- Founder of the state of Rhodesia in Africa
- While in South Africa, he formed his own mining company, De Beers Consolidated Mines. Today, De Beers is perhaps best known for its diamonds.

Source: *South Africa. - ppt download* [48]

Cecil made his fortunes plundering the African continent. In the new colonies, he carved out and sucked dry of every diamond he could find. Additionally, in unrelated news, the De Beers diamond company was busted working with the Nazis in the past (embezzling supply to the Axis and helping Hitler with his schemes for a global diamond monopoly as well as denying the Allied powers enough).

Again, everything old is new again. Many African officials have equated De Beers' modern operations to slavery. They exploit schemes and subvert transparency initiatives with loopholes such as the Kimberly process (a well-intentioned, but ineffective way to try to increase the ethics of diamond mining) to keep a steady supply of blood diamonds coming (since Africa has 65% of mined diamonds, but more on that later). As long as their money doesn't go *directly* to warlords and terrorists, they can claim their products are ethically mined (even if their only one or two steps down the chain of their production from them).

What few protections there are in the dirty trade of diamonds are avoided and subverted if not openly opposed by foreign powers (like Russia trying to remove certain protections). De Beers was banned from the U.S. for some 50 years, but the shady, privately traded cartel is back now. Yay.

When De Beers did the shooting themselves, there was coercion or of course the more traditional method. Now the terrorist warlords and the finance do all the work for them, and they can kick back and let the cash roll in.

There are many other examples like De Beers who could thrive in the transition from classic to new colonialism. All this was facilitated through corporate influence, so they could transform young African nations into client states.

The main method of implementing these destructive policies for De Beers and its ilk to thrive is the IMF and WB's Structural Adjustment Programs also known as SAPs. SAPs are predatory loans from the IMF or World Bank with the intent to influence economies detrimentally for the nation in question but beneficially for foreign countries. The idea is that if the African countries bend the knee to the modern Empires of the world, they can get some leftovers to keep them barely alive.

However, said foreign powers sell these sink-hole plans as ways to, *"adjust the country's economic structure, improve international competitiveness, and restore its balance of payments. ...SAPs are supposedly intended to balance the government's budget, reduce inflation, and stimulate economic growth."*[49] That is how they tricked many countries into signing on and sealing their fates.

When in fact, they really mean this:

Decrease government spending
* Lay off workers (mostly health and education)
* Cut government programs (education, health, agriculture)
* End subsidies for poor (food, transport, housing, water)

Improve terms for foreign investment & increase exports
* Reduce taxation, currency controls on investors
* Devalue currency
* Reduce or freeze wages – reduce worker power

Privatize economy "Free Market Rules"
* Market regulation of prices (huge increases)
* "willingness to pay" ethic for social services
* Growth of private health care

Reschedule debt over longer period (indefinite)

Source: *Debt Structural Adjustment Programs*
SAPs and Primary Health [50]

In reality, this modern form of colonization (SAPs) minimizes a government's ability to maintain national sovereignty and assure they look out for their own nation's interest. Instead, other western powers dictate policy that is to their benefit and rarely carry the positive benefits to Africa that were promised. Surprising no one, since a main condition for many SAPs, is a cut to social spending and wages, the poor are the greatest victims. The very same impoverished people that SAPs are supposed to help.

Additionally, the loans are often given as payments to deal with former loans and so on in an eternal cycle. From there private companies come in from 'foreign investors' who pay next to no taxes, so they extract resources and leave nothing but scraps.

It is also a pay-to-win system since whoever donates the most to the World Bank gets to have incredible amounts of influence on SAPs (in unrelated news the United States as the largest donor has 17.25% of the votes of the World Bank and *every* World Bank President ever has been an American. Also, they have 17.46% of the IMF).

And all of that is just the start. These deals open the floodgates to all the other kinds of exploitation that will be discussed next.

Even the World Bank thinks that the World Bank sucks. In a report on their SAPs, the World Bank concluded alongside several others that their programs to 'help' Africa have in fact led to, *"expanding poverty, inequality, and insecurity around the world. [They have] torn at the heart of economies and the social 6 Canadian Centre for Policy Alternatives fabric... increasing tensions among different social strata, fueling extremist movements, and delegitimizing democratic political systems."* [51]

The IMF uses a technique called coercion. Coercion means:

There are two types—implicit and explicit. The IMF couldn't be caught explicitly threatening countries so instead uses implicit methods to capitalize on their vulnerable situations.

The IMF coerces the countries by only giving financial aid in exchange for reducing labour standards. They have to make it easier for foreign companies to come in, but not as fellow competitors in a fair market. Instead, they are monopolies that choke out local business and coerce native labourers into extracting their nations' wealth to send it overseas.

Many claim they have come to help but 'liberalizing the economy' isn't necessarily good. One of the main components of that is *deregulation*. This leads to those same sweatshops and dangerous conditions that the countries later look down on African nations for having.

Things got even worse under the tenure of the eternal friend of all African people: US President Ronald Reagan. He thought the Southern countries were doing too well and so put into action plans to fully destroy them. In summary, to quote a research paper on the subject: *"The Reagan Administration came into office in 1980 determined to discipline an increasingly independent Third World and make it serve U.S."*

While military interventions or 'low-intensity conflicts' were the main way western powers dealt with uppity nations in South America and the Middle East (like Angola, Nicaragua, Panama, and Grenada, and against liberation movements in El Salvador, Guatemala, and the Philippines.)

For Africa, they had a different scheme. An economic approach that in 1988 was even admitted by the Presidential Commission of Integrated Long-Term Strategy, *"We ... need to think of low-intensity conflict as a form of warfare that is not a problem just for the Department of Defense. In many situations, the United States will need not just DoD personnel and material but diplomats and information specialists, agricultural chemists, bankers, and economists ... and scores of other professionals."*

And that is just American shenaniganry. Throw a dart at a map in the global North and there are bound to be some guilty parties snickering at the profits they made off with like bandits.

Many governments also participate in this process so they can skim money off the top. Like the Sambo in Uncle Tom's Cabin, these Sambos aid companies in robbing Africa blind.

This is the result.

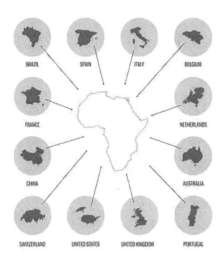

A sample of countries with companies implicated in foreign bribery in Africa (source: Exporting Corruption, 2019)

Source: _Exporting Corruption_ [52]

Champion of Financial Neocolonialism: France

Disclaimer! Disclaimer! Disclaimer!!!

The people of France are not the nation of France. The devious stuff the French government gets up to is not their fault and many of them don't even know any of this. Average French people are not at fault for this only the architects of this system and the cheap bureaucrats who continue to perpetuate this plundering of Africa.

But I'd be remiss to talk about neo-Colonialism without an appropriate case study. Even surpassing the United States of America, France is arguably the most effective western neocolonial power when it comes to Africa.

Ah, the French Neocolonialism… it's often been celebrated for its Machiavellian deviousness.

The main mode of manipulation is through currency control using the CFA franc. CFA used to be a direct reminder of who was in charge since it meant, *Colonies françaises d'Afrique* or French colonies of Africa. Then they changed the name to a more euphemistic, *Communauté française d'Afrique*, French

Community of Africa. They were a community, but they were still *French*.

Nonetheless, the CFA France is a currency issued and controlled by the French government. Member states of the CFA are beholden to France in their economic policies and as a result, are perpetually aligned with French economic interests. The rules were made by France and were clearly rigged in their favour. The four main rules they established were:

"Firstly, a fixed rate of exchange with the euro (and previously the French franc) set at 1 euro = 655.957 CFA francs. Secondly, a French guarantee of the unlimited convertibility of CFA francs into euros. Thirdly, a centralisation of foreign exchange reserves. Since 2005, the two central banks – the Central Bank of West African States (BCEAO) and the Bank of Central African States (BEAC) – have been required to deposit 50 percent of their foreign exchange reserves in a special French Treasury 'operating account.' Immediately following independence, this figure stood at 100 percent (and from 1973 to 2005, at 65 per cent). This arrangement is a quid pro quo for the French 'guarantee' of convertibility. The accords stipulate that foreign exchange reserves

must exceed money in circulation by a margin of 20 percent. Before the fall in oil prices, the money supply coverage rate (the ratio of foreign exchange reserves to money in circulation) consistently approached 100 percent, implying in theory that Africans could dispense with the French 'guarantee.' The final pillar of the CFA franc, is the principle of free capital transfer within the franc zone."

But don't worry, France has finally allowed its humble servants to be free of the CFA Franc. There are now plans to ditch the old colonial relic and then… get a new obviously rigged, France-controlled currency called the Eco by 2027. Nice.

A former French President said it best when he gave the game away and admitted:

"We drained Africa for 4 and a half centuries. Next, we plundered its raw materials. After that, we said: they (Africans) are good for nothing. In the name of religion, we destroyed their culture and now, as we have to act with elegance, we are picking their brains with scholarships. Thereupon, we are claiming that the unfortunate Africa is not in a brilliant condition and is not making elites. Having enriched on its back, we are now lecturing."

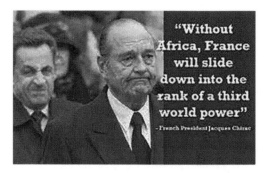

"Without Africa, France will slide down into the rank of a third world power"

- French President Jacques Chirac

Source: *African Revolt on Twitter: "Jacques Chirac: Without Africa, France will slide down into the rank of a third world...."* [53]

To wit, he summed things up nicely with, *"We have to be honest, and acknowledge that a big part of the money in our banks comes precisely from the exploitation of the African continent."* And it is pretty accurate.

Despite pulling out of Africa, France can still have many former colonies dancing their tune through numerous avenues of control. If any of those fail, France has thousands of troops stationed in their former colonies to keep them in line. Hate to say it, but colonialism isn't quite over yet.

Water and Land Exploitation

Another resource of Africa being exploited by foreign interests is land and water.

Another interesting note is constant reminders of Africa's lack of clean drinking water (though never specific as to where in Africa and always showing the most extreme patronizing example). They never think to ask, *"What polluted the water, to begin with?"*

Now Africa is home to many of the oldest settlements of humans on Earth and so as the development of civilization tells us: they must have had viable water supplies. But look at them today (examples of polluted water):

Source: *South Africa has failed to protect locals from gold mine pollution: Harvard report - MINING.COM* [54]

Source: *Africa's Exploding Plastic Nightmare* [55]

Africa did not come packaged with pollution; humans did this to it. Corporate and industrial waste churns out profit for large corporations but also spews out toxic waste to pollute drinking supplies.

In Ethiopia, about 90 percent of industries do not have any kind of treatment plant and discharge their solid and liquid wastes untreated into the environment. In Ghana, about 60 percent of water bodies are polluted with the main sources being illegal mining activities, industrial waste, household disposals and farming. In South Africa, there is also an estimated annual release of about 93,000 metric tons of industrial waste into the Zambezi River. And in Tanzania, the volume of wastewater generated by industries is 683,717 cubic meters per day … Food processing and textile industries are the major water polluting industries in Tanzania and Ghana. And so on for almost everywhere on the continent. This is *not* natural; this is either negligence or contempt. For the part of companies, they need to get their waste under control and corrupt government officials who look the other way and don't enforce environmental protections or laws should also be held accountable.

Other continents are very wasteful as well, but because of the care taken to invest in infrastructure alongside this harm, the effects are lessened. When the profits of businesses stay in countries, they can make money *and* save their citizens. In fact, surprise, surprise, in North America this is even done with a profit motive. North America Waste Management Market to Generate $229.3 Billion by 2027 because of course. If even half the consideration was given to Africa the industries could at least be somewhat more ethically sourced and operated.

As such, Africa takes the lion's share of the negative effects of industrialization as the development required for wealth extraction remains within the private sector of foreign investors and rarely gets handed over to the people who could invest in the same commodities that we take for granted in western and Asian countries.

The negative effects of industrial water pollution are:

1. UNEP has found that a full 28 percent of Africa's disease burden is a result of environmental factors such as contaminated water, which causes diarrheal disease, and air pollution which causes respiratory illness.

2. Surface water pollution makes securing groundwater a necessity, but drilling is expensive, and the maintenance is no small feat either

3. Even underground wells can be polluted which are a major source of water so all those well-building charities better also test water purity before celebrating

4. Young children die from dehydration and malnutrition, as a result of suffering from diarrheal illnesses that could be prevented by clean water and good hygiene. Diseases

such as cholera are spread rampantly during the wet season.

5. Women and young girls, who are the major role-players in accessing and carrying water, are prevented from doing income-generating work or attending school, as the majority of their day is often spent walking miles for their daily water needs.

So, the next time one of those ads comes on with sad African children near polluted water, suffering you should be under no illusion that it is 'just how it is in Africa.' Know that up the hill there is bound to be some foreign company's factory spewing out enough waste to choke a nation.

And there are plans by industries (mainly oil corporations) to make the practice even worse! The main target is Kenya, an exemplary example of nations trying to be responsible and ethical with their environment. However, since 2018 China has refused to take their garbage so many international companies have spied Africa as their new dumping ground. To them, Kenya's attempt to mitigate the negative impacts of industrializing won't do. Now the idea is to crush

Kenya's progress and use them as a practice ground for a scheme to be spread to other African countries!

"They want Kenya to reverse its strict limits on plastics, including the 2017 plastic bag ban! It's a No!" tweeted James Wakibia, who pushed hard for Kenya's plastic bag ban. He is now campaigning for all East African countries to ban *"all unnecessary single-use plastic."*

Best of luck there.

While foreign companies try to crush Kenya, other nations should look to them as a shining example. Their measures being taken as well as a few others can greatly help.

Here are some proposed solutions to the Water Crises:

- Education to change consumption/lifestyle
- Innovation in water conservation technologies
- Recycling/water treatment systems
- Improved irrigation technologies / agricultural practices
- Appropriate pricing/water rights markets
- Energy-efficient desalination plants

- Water catchment/harvesting
- Community-based governance / partnerships
- Better government policies/regulations
- Holistic management of ecosystems
- Improved distribution infrastructure
- Corporate water foot-printing / sustainable manufacturing
- International policy frameworks / institutional cooperation
- Address pollution to improve the quality of water
- Public common resources / equitable access
- Research & Development / Innovation
- Water projects in developing countries/ transfer of technology
- Climate change mitigation
- Population growth control

Rwanda is another good example of progress being made in Africa that is both extremely exemplary and commendable. Slowly but surely resistance to environmental destruction can be successful and Africa can be saved.

While African nations do their parts to fix the problem… we should probably stop letting foreign interests cause them in the first place.

Human Resources (Labour)

Basically, slave labour. No regulations. Thanks, IMF. However, they can hide the negative consequences and continue to insist that these policies are essential for Africa to keep foreign investment and by putting out propaganda like the *Doing Business* publication they pretend it is helping. It's really bad.

In Africa, there are sweatshops where people are paid as low as 5 pounds a week (you can find their handiwork at your local H&M if you're interested).

One such provision most countries do without as a result is child labour restrictions.

Table 1.3   Children Ten to Fourteen Years Old in Labor Force by African Region, 1992

	Number of Working Children	Percentage of African Child Workers	Percentage of Working Children
Eastern Africa	7,965,000	50.7	32.9
Western Africa	5,785,000	36.9	24.2
Middle Africa	1,848,000	11.8	21.6
Southern Africa	100,000	0.6	4.6

Sources: Adapted from Christiaan Grootaert and Ravi Kanbur, *Child Labor: A Review,* Working Paper no. 1454 (Washington, D.C.: World Bank, 1995) and based on International Labour Organization (ILO) and International Program on the Elimination of Child Labour (IPEC), *Implementation Report 1992–93* (Geneva: ILO-IPEC, 1993): (1) results of a special ILO questionnaire sent to more than 200 countries and territories in April 1992, (2) the LABORSTAT database, (3) preliminary ILO estimates and projections of the economically active population, and (4) United Nations, *Sex and Age Distribution of the World's Population, 1950–2025* (New York: United Nations Population Division, 1992).

An analysis of the Exploitation of Children in Africa yielded these horrifying results:

> *The abuse and exploitation of children is a major public policy priority for all African countries. Throughout the continent, children are routinely abused and exploited as sex objects; tools in the production of various goods, including cocoa, gold, and various minerals, as well as, services, such as pornography and prostitution; and, as child soldiers to fight in sectarian conflicts and civil wars. Children in Africa are exploited and abused by both domestic and external or foreign actors and these include, but are not limited to, family members and community leaders, foreign tourists who seek the continent's children for sex, and international criminal gangs who are engaged in the production of child pornography, sex trafficking and the illegal harvesting and sale of organs. With respect to the use of African children in military conflicts, exploiters include state- and non-state actors. In several African countries, religious and customary practices account for a significant amount of the abuse that children, particularly girl children, are subjected to. In addition, many children are also subjected to servitude labor in cocoa plantations, mines, traditional religious shrines, and the homes of rich urban dwellers. International actors involved in the abuse and exploitation of African children also include UN peacekeepers and aid workers belonging to various non-governmental organizations. Effectively combatting the abuse and exploitation of African children must begin with*

Source: *Child Exploitation* [56]

The response to this epidemic of child exploitation is often passivity. Since many people assume, that's just African culture. This ignores the fact that child labour wasn't properly banned until 1938 in the United States and 1933 in the United Kingdom. The nations were still industrializing as many African countries are now (on account of most only being around 50 years old which is *very* young for countries).

The nature of child labour is intertwined with other economic woes which among other things are caused by, *"In addition to poverty, lack of resources, together with other factors such as credit constraints, income shocks, school quality, and parental attitudes toward education are all associated with child labour."*

Many factors can be addressed in Africa, but things such as credit constraints and income shocks sound an awful lot like SAP shenanigans, don't they?

Effects of SAPs

- Enormously increased food, transport prices
- Huge levels of unemployment
- Non-living wage for those who remain working ($20-40 per month)
- User fees for health, education, and other services
- Reduction in education, health care quality
- Social unrest – demonstrations, riots

Source: *Debt Structural Adjustment Programs SAPs and Primary Health* [57]

SAPs most heavily impact the African people in terms of regulation or lack thereof that comes from the condition of loans. Additionally, high interest can discourage people from taking out loans to start their own businesses and instead force people to work for foreign companies if they hope to survive. The 'market reforms' make it harder for employees to become owners and keep many from succeeding.

Natural Resources (oil, gold, etc.)

As the historian, Walter Rodney said, *"When citizens of Europe own the land and the mines of Africa, this is the most direct way of sucking the African continent."* Western companies seem to see Africa as a giant piggy bank of natural resources. And boy howdy are there a lot of natural resources.

Source: *The Sobering Truth About Africa's "Resource Wealth" – The Afro Optimist* [58]

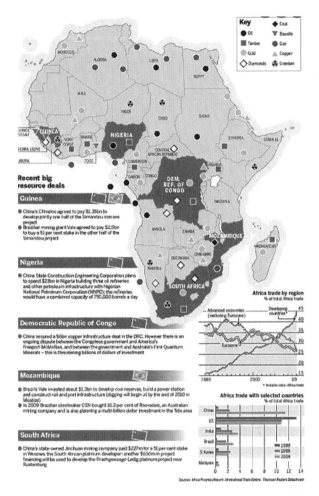

Source: <u>*Africa Natural Resources - Environment for Kids*</u> [52]

Africa has so many resources that the other continents have become fabulously rich from. And from the fine folks at the IMF here is the wealth of nations, totalled up by continent:

List by the International Monetary Fund (2021 estimate)[3]

Rank ⬍	Continent ⬍	GDP (US$billion) ⬍	Share (%) ⬍
	World	93,864	100.0
1	Asia	36,383	38.8
2	North America	26,298	28.0
3	Europe	23,614	25.2
4	South America	3,019	3.2
5	Africa	2,601	2.8
6	Oceania	1,894	2.0
7	Far Eastern Asia	23,625	25.2
	Unaccounted	55	0.1

Source: _World Economic Outlook (April 2021) - GDP, current prices_ [60]

For being the richest continent in terms of natural resources, this disparity should be alarming.

Now natural resources aren't everything, manufacturing, and the processing of raw materials always (conveniently) pays better than simply extracting and selling said natural resources. But such a discrepancy is so noticeable it trumps even those qualifiers or potential excuses for it. Surprisingly, according to the United Nations: Africa is home to some 30 percent of the world's mineral reserves, eight percent of the world's natural gas and 12 percent of the world's oil reserves. The continent has 40 percent of the world's gold and up to 90 percent of its chromium and platinum. The largest reserves of cobalt, diamonds, platinum, and uranium in the world are in Africa. It holds 65 percent of the world's arable land and ten percent of the planet's internal renewable fresh water source.

Now most surprising to many people there is probably Africa's possession of 65% of the world's arable (farmable) land. *More than half.* All the western images of desolate deserts and derelict valleys don't seem to align expectations with reality (or the sheer number of famines Africa faces)

Though many try to downplay this level of exploitation and to keep their eyes off of what is happening there. Sometimes with the help of a useful Sambo or two. For example, during research for this project, an antithesis was found in an article by the IMANI Center for Policy and Education. Despite the name, they are a proud, self-identifying Think Tank (hack frauds who do 'research' to promote agendas for corporate interests) in Ghana. They are however in truth the stooges of an American think tank the Atlas Institute, a pro-neo-colonial crazy libertarian group (with money from the Rockefellers thrown in). But that is not to say their deceptive writings are of low quality. In fact, it is well written and convincing so it would be useful to analyze them as an example.

But enough poisoning the well. Their contrary beliefs deserve fair consideration. The best opposition to this idea comes from a Rockefeller-funded think tank puff piece that intentionally misconstrues facts to try and debunk the amount of Africa's wealth.

The article and its ill intentionally misconstrue a continent's natural resource reserves with how much they export each year. A key example is to argue that South Africa's gold reserves are overstated because in fact they are only the 4th largest natural gold producer with China easily taking the number one spot. This is true. This is also completely irrelevant since the argument made would also include the untapped gold reserves sitting under Johannesburg (the Witwatersrand gold reserves which are the largest of their kind in the world) and all over the country.

Be on guard for people who argue about 'gold mine reserves' or 'gold exported' since these are *not* measurements of what is actually in the ground, but instead a measurement of the economic values. Many words sound similar but are not the same thing when it comes to natural resource quantities. *So,* for simplicity, Australia, as a country, has the most gold in the ground. And the continent of Africa has the most gold in the ground as a continent. South Africa alone is touted as, *"Today the world's unmined reserves are estimated at 1 billion troy oz (31 billion grams), about half in the Witwatersrand area of the Republic of South Africa."* Most lists that don't include Africa do so because they are counting 'gold mine reserves' or 'gold production.' If Person A has 10 coconuts but only gives away 1, and Person B has 5 coconuts and gives away 4, Person B does NOT have 4 times as many coconuts as Person A. At least, that is my understanding of the odd confusion and contradiction in researching the topic as it pertains to gold (apologies for the tangent, but people are very insistent in trying to 'debunk' Africa's gold reserves for some reason).

The fact that they lay there unused only reinforces Africa being unable to reach its full potential in the interest of not flooding the market with excess resources (it is there but not extracted, likely for fear of lowering prices due to supply and demand). Also, articles like this are very tricky with word choices so be sure to fact-check *everything* to ensure it is not misleading or an outright lie.

On the topic of South Africa, the country's incredible gold reserves paradoxically lay mostly unmined. Despite gold mining being the literal thing on which many cities like Johannesburg were founded, due to industrial decline, much of it remains unused. Being used and then dumped by foreign mining interests has led to ruin and an increase in crime. Many sensibly figure it is better to illegally mine the gold there for money, rather than steal from others in the community instead. Imagine, all the prosperity and good that would come from a thriving industry in South Africa if the people could have control over their own resources and profit off of it (without the exploitation this time). That way communities could continue thriving and avoid the nightmare scenario of foreign interest drying up and leaving the community out to dry when they are done with them.

Companies come to Africa and extract what they want but couldn't be bothered to invest in the infrastructure of the people living there. Classic examples are factories that dump tons of filth and pollution into African water but don't even pay a second thought to building accommodating water treatment or sewage plants that ensure the environment can survive the toll of their operations.

But there's no profit motive in that and the domestic negative impacts have no way of materially harming the company financially so there is no incentive for them to clean up their act- *and the environment*. Most people in the nations where the products are bought, and the stocks are traded either don't know or don't care about the negative impacts, so they get away Scot-free.

Congo for example has enormous wealth in natural resources but none of it is for the natives.

Companies come in and exploit the government to only pay 5% of the taxes owed. They plunder the land and make off like bandits while leaving ruined environments.

Conclusion

All of this exploitation and corruption can have extremely destabilizing effects on a region that can and *have* ruined lives. Apologies will not help alleviate these real-world issues; action will. And the first act of reconciling is not to 'feel guilty' but instead to stop. This book does not advocate for any feelings of guilt, feelings are irrelevant here. If there are any prescriptions to be taken from all this then let it be that from A to Z, from Angola to Zimbabwe these predatory schemes must be exposed and expelled from the African continent! These problems may seem distant or even unimportant to some but remember in the words of Dr. Martin Luther King Jr. *"injustice anywhere is a threat to justice everywhere."* The perpetrators of such things are not only *Enemies of Africa* but Enemies of the World!

Index

A

Africa Natural Resources, 152
African Union, 120, 121
Alexander H. Stephens, 40
Alexander the Great, 119
Algeria, 125
All Lives Matter, 68
Antebellum South, 19
Anti-Semitic, 65, 68
Asante, Molefi Kete, 23
Atlas Institute, 155

B

Bacon, Francis, 98
Bank of Central African
    States (BEAC), 137
Barca, Hannibal, 117
Battle of Hayes Pond, 51,
    56, 58
Battle of Liberty Place, 44
Bell, Alexander Graham, 107
Birth of a Nation, 49, 50
Black Armed Guard, 53, 54
Black Lives Matter, 69

Branding, 34, 35
British Phrenological Society,
    105
Brown, Will, 47
Burning, 36, 50, 55

C

Central Bank of West African
    States (BCEAO), 137
Chattel Slavery, 22, 23
Child exploitation, 149
China, 144, 155
Churchill, Winston, 107
Civil Rights Movement, 121
Cole, James Catfish, 51, 52,
    53, 55, 56
Colonialism, 74, 75, 76, 77,
    79, 80, 93, 125, 130,
    136, 139
Colonies françaises dAfrique
    (CFA), 136
Confederacy, 40, 41, 42
Crowe, James R., 42
Cultural Marxism, 68
Cyrus the Great, 18

References

[1] Asante, Molefi Kete (2012). *The African American People: A Global History*, Routledge

[2] Little, Becky. "Details of Brutal First Slave Voyages Discovered - HISTORY." *HISTORY*, www.history.com, 21 Mar. 2019, https://www.history.com/news/transatlantic-slave-first-ships-details.

[3] Exert from Atlantic World Encounters, Meguerian.org. http://meguerian.org/wp-content/uploads/2012/02/Slave-Trade.pdf

[4] "Trans-Atlantic - Introductory Maps." *Trans-Atlantic - Introductory Maps*, www.slavevoyages.org, https://www.slavevoyages.org/voyage/maps#introductory-.

[5] "Liverpool's Slave Trade Legacy | History Today." *Liverpool's Slave Trade Legacy | History Today*, www.historytoday.com, https://www.historytoday.com/history-matters/liverpool%E2%80%99s-slave-trade-legacy.

[6] Jones, Jae. "Branding of Slaves: Brutal Act Used for Identification Purposes and Severe Punishment | Black Then." *Black Then*, blackthen.com, 8 Feb. 2020, https://blackthen.com/branding-of-slaves-brutal-act-used-for-identification-purposes-and-severe-punishment/.

[7] 'Barbarities in the West Indias [Indies]' - National Portrait Gallery." *NPG D12417; "Barbarities in the West Indias [Indies]" - Portrait - National Portrait Gallery*, www.npg.org.uk, https://www.npg.org.uk/collections/search/portrait/mw61443/Barbarities-in-the-West-Indias-Indies.

[8] "El Ku Klux Klan Que Nació En Nochebuena." *La Vanguardia*, www.lavanguardia.com, 24 Dec. 2020, https://www.lavanguardia.com/historiayvida/historia-contemporanea/20201224/6144256/ku-klux-klan-nochebuena-origen.html.

[9] @politico. "KKK Chapter to Hold Rally on South Carolina Statehouse Grounds." *KKK Chapter to Hold Rally on South Carolina Statehouse Grounds*, www.politico.com, 29 June 2015, https://www.politico.com/story/2015/06/kkk-chapter-north-carolina-rally-south-carolina-statehouse-confederate-flag-119548.

[10] "A Political Cartoon by Thomas Nast Titled 'The Union as It Was,' Published in *Harper's Weekly* October 24, 1874. | DPLA." *A Political Cartoon by Thomas Nast Titled "The Union as It Was," Published in *Harper's Weekly* October 24, 1874. | DPLA*, dp.la, https://dp.la/primary-source-sets/ida-b-wells-and-anti-lynching-activism/sources/1118.

[11] "EDITOR'S NOTE: No More 'Lynching Logic' to Excuse Brutality Against Black People." *EDITOR'S NOTE: No More 'Lynching Logic' to Excuse Brutality Against Black People | Jackson Free Press | Jackson, MS*, www.jacksonfreepress.com, https://www.jacksonfreepress.com/news/2020/sep/02/editors-note-no-more-lynching-logic-excuse-brutali/.

[12] "MOSH Exhibit On America's History Of Lynching Opens Saturday | WJCT News." *WJCT News*, news.wjct.org, 22

Aug. 2019, https://news.wjct.org/first-coast/2019-08-22/mosh-exhibit-on-americas-history-of-lynching-opens-saturday.

[13] ("'The NAACP's Silent Parade' 1917 Suite | Blackbird V16n2 | #gallery") Full Citation:"'The NAACP's Silent Parade' 1917 Suite | Blackbird V16n2 | #gallery." *The NAACP's Silent Parade" 1917 Suite | Blackbird V16n2 | #gallery*, blackbird. vcu.edu, https://blackbird.vcu.edu/v16n2/gallery/1917/intro_page.shtml.

[14] ("Tulsa Race Massacre of 1921 | Commission, Facts, & Books") Full Citation:"Tulsa Race Massacre of 1921 | Commission, Facts, & Books." *Encyclopedia Britannica*, www.britannica.com, https://www.britannica.com/event/Tulsa-race-massacre-of-1921.

[15] "The Most Iconic Photographs of All Time - LIFE." *LIFE*, time.com, http://time.com/section/life/.

[16] "Native America Today | ⚜ The Battle of Hayes Pond: How Indian Country Defeated the KKK." *Native America Today*, nativeamericatoday.com, 13 Dec. 2017, https://nativeamericatoday.com/the-battle-of-hayes-pond/.

[17] Telegram, RockyMount. "Rockymounttelegram.Com." *RockyMount Telegram*, www.rockymounttelegram.com, 13 Aug. 2022, http://www.rockymounttelegram.com/.

[18] "File:Battle of Hayes Pond Sign.Jpg - Wikimedia Commons." *File:Battle of Hayes Pond Sign.Jpg - Wikimedia Commons*, commons.wikimedia.org, 17 Aug. 2020, https://commons.wikimedia.org/wiki/File:Battle_of_Hayes_pond_sign.jpg.

[19] Lartey, Jamiles, and Sam Morris. "How White Americans Used Lynchings to Terrorize and Control Black People | Race | The Guardian." *The Guardian*, www.theguardian.com, 26 Apr.

2018, https://www.theguardian.com/us-news/2018/apr/26/
lynchings-memorial-us-south-montgomery-alabama.

[20] McArdle, Terence. "Decades before the Unite the Right
Rally, 30,000 White Supremacists in Klan Robes Marched
in Washington - The Washington Post." *Washington Post*,
www.washingtonpost.com, 17 Aug. 2017, https://www.
washingtonpost.com/news/retropolis/wp/2017/08/17/the-
day-30000-white-supremacists-in-kkk-robes-marched-in-the-
nations-capital/.

[21] "Martin Luther King, Jr. -- I'm Black and Beautiful."
YouTube, youtu.be, 20 Apr. 2008, https://youtu.be/
nGLF0X3WIiE.

[22] "Difference between Imperialism and
Colonialism | Imperialism vs. Colonialism."
Difference Betweenz, differencebetweenz.com,
16 Oct. 2017, https://differencebetweenz.com/
difference-between-imperialism-and-colonialism/

[23] "THE SCRAMBLE FOR AFRICA Essential Question
What Was." *THE SCRAMBLE FOR AFRICA Essential
Question What Was*, slidetodoc.com, https://slidetodoc.com/
the-scramble-for-africa-essential-question-what-was/.

[24] J.P. Waldie, Dr Derek. "THE BERLIN CONFERENCE ON
AFRICA 1884-1885 (Vc)." *THE BERLIN CONFERENCE
ON AFRICA 1884-1885 (Vc)*, www.timewisetraveller.co.uk,
https://www.timewisetraveller.co.uk/berlin2.html.

[25] @MatadorNetwork. "This Is What Africa Looked Like Before
European Colonialism." *Matador Network*, matadornetwork.
com, 25 Nov. 2017, https://matadornetwork.com/read/
mapped-africa-scramble-africa/.

26 "Atlantic Slave Trade: Fallacy of Blacks Selling Blacks."
    YouTube, youtu.be, 23 Oct. 2016, https://youtu.be/
    pJ5zizWjSko.

27 "File:Maps Global Slavery Index 2019.Png - Wikimedia
    Commons." *File:Maps Global Slavery Index 2019.Png -
    Wikimedia Commons*, commons.wikimedia.org, 13 Aug. 2020,
    https://commons.wikimedia.org/wiki/File:Maps_Global_
    Slavery_Index_2019.png.

28 "Top 10 World History Lessons Ideas and Inspiration."
    Pinterest, www.pinterest.ca, https://www.pinterest.ca/ideas/
    world-history-lessons/960978271654/.

29 "Africa Is Not a Country | Bill Clinton | The Guardian." *The
    Guardian*, www.theguardian.com, 24 Jan. 2014, https://www.
    theguardian.com/world/2014/jan/24/africa-clinton.

30 Lapite, Shade. "Mansa Musa: Glitter and Gold, Streaming
    Now...." *Coffee Bookshelves*, coffeebookshelves.com,
    13 Feb. 2020, https://coffeebookshelves.com/2020/02/13/
    mansa-musa-glitter-and-gold-streaming-now/

31 "Royal Residences | Windsor Castle - Royal.Uk." *The Royal
    Family*, www.royal.uk, 21 Dec. 2015, https://www.royal.uk/
    royal-residences-windsor-castle.

32 "Great Zimbabwe | World Pilgrimage Guide, www.
    sacredsites.com, https://sacredsites.com/africa/zimbabwe/
    great_zimbabwe_ruins.html.

33 "Nick Fuentes and the African Wheel." *YouTube*, youtu.be, 2
    Aug. 2020, https://youtu.be/ry2cRP73h9s.

34 "10 Facts About General Robert E. Lee." *History Hit*, www.
    historyhit.com, 23 Sept. 2021, https://www.historyhit.com/
    facts-about-general-robert-e-lee/.

[35] "The Five Races of Mankind According to This German Poster, 1911 - Rare Historical Photos." *Rare Historical Photos*, rarehistoricalphotos.com, 26 Aug. 2014, https://rarehistoricalphotos.com/five-races-of-mankind-1911/.

[36] "Steps of the Scientific Method." *Science Buddies*, www.sciencebuddies.org, https://www.sciencebuddies.org/science-fair-projects/science-fair/steps-of-the-scientific-method.

[37] Wills, Matthew. "Walt Whitman, America's Phrenologist - JSTOR Daily." *JSTOR Daily*, daily.jstor.org, 31 May 2019, https://daily.jstor.org/walt-whitman-americas-phrenologist/.

[38] "Writing de Jure » History of Criminology." *Writing de Jure » History of Criminology*, writingdejure.web.unc.edu, https://writingdejure.web.unc.edu/resources/history-of-criminology/.

[39] "The Illustrated Self-Instructor in Phrenology and Physiology: With over One Hundred Engravings: Together with the Chart and Character of ... as Marked by ...: Fowler, O. S. (Orson Squire), 1809-1887: Free Download, Borrow, and Streaming: Internet Archive." *Internet Archive*, archive.org, https://archive.org/details/7703816.nlm.nih.gov/page/n15/mode/2up?view=theater.

[40] "Phrenology and 'Scientific Racism' in the 19th Century | Real Archaeology." *Phrenology and "Scientific Racism" in the 19th Century | Real Archaeology*, pages.vassar.edu, 5 Mar. 2017, https://pages.vassar.edu/realarchaeology/2017/03/05/phrenology-and-scientific-racism-in-the-19th-century/

[41] "No. 2148 American Phrenology." *No. 2148 American Phrenology*, www.uh.edu, https://www.uh.edu/engines/epi2148.htm.

42 "The Bell Curve." *YouTube*, youtu.be, 3 Dec. 2019, https://
    youtu.be/UBc7qBS1Ujo.

43 "The Bell Curve." *YouTube*, youtu.be, 3 Dec. 2019, https://
    youtu.be/UBc7qBS1Ujo.

44 Stalin, Weber, Islam, White Ethnics, Adorno, Prejudgement,
    Thomas,. "The Social Meaning of Race & Ethnicity - Ppt
    Download." *The Social Meaning of Race & Ethnicity -
    Ppt Download*, slideplayer.com, https://slideplayer.com/
    slide/14340801/.

45 "IQ Classification - Wikipedia." *IQ Classification - Wikipedia*,
    en.wikipedia.org, 4 Aug. 2008, https://en.wikipedia.org/wiki/
    IQ_classification.

46 Maranzani, Barbara. "Martin Luther King Jr. and
    Malcolm X Only Met Once." *Biography*, www.biography.
    com, 19 Jan. 2021, https://www.biography.com/news/
    martin-luther-king-jr-malcolm-x-meeting.

47 "Objective 11- Antharya." *Objective 11- Antharya - Chapter
    37*, shropchapter37.weebly.com, http://shropchapter37.weebly.
    com/objective-11--antharya.html.

48 Cecil Rhodes, De Beers, Kruger, Nelson, de Klerk, Hope,
    Laws, Nelson Mandela. "South Africa. - Ppt Download."
    South Africa. - Ppt Download, slideplayer.com, https://
    slideplayer.com/slide/6147393/

49 "Structural Adjustment - Wikipedia." *Structural Adjustment
    - Wikipedia*, en.wikipedia.org, 1 Feb. 2013, https://
    en.wikipedia.org/wiki/Structural_adjustment.

50 "Debt Structural Adjustment Programs SAPs and Primary
    Health." *Debt Structural Adjustment Programs SAPs and
    Primary Health*, slidetodoc.com, https://slidetodoc.com/
    debt-structural-adjustment-programs-saps-and-primary-health/.

[51] https://documents1.worldbank.org/curated/en/879521468188667488/text/100230-PUB-Box393220B-PUBLIC-PUBDATE-10-14-2015-DOI-10-1596-978-1-4648-0703-9-EPI-210703.txt

[52] "JavaScript Не е Налице." *Twitter*, twitter.com, https://twitter.com/transparencitng/status/1149369661563314176?lang=bg

[53] https://twitter.com/africarevolt/status/1221507678591168513

[54] "South Africa Has Failed to Protect Locals from Gold Mine Pollution: Harvard Report - MINING.COM." *MINING.COM*, www.mining.com, 12 Oct. 2016, https://www.mining.com/south-africa-has-failed-to-protect-locals-from-gold-mine-pollution-harvard-report/.

[55] "Africa's Exploding Plastic Nightmare - Greenpeace Africa." *Greenpeace Africa*, www.greenpeace.org, https://www.greenpeace.org/africa/en/blogs/11125/africas-exploding-plastic-nightmare/

[56] "The Rule of Law and the Exploitation of Children in Africa 42 Hastings International and Comparative Law Review 2019." *HeinOnline*, heinonline.org, 8 Mar. 2021, https://heinonline.org/HOL/LandingPage?handle=hein.journals/hasint42&div=10&id=&page=.

[57] "Debt Structural Adjustment Programs SAPs and Primary Health." *Debt Structural Adjustment Programs SAPs and Primary Health*, slidetodoc.com, https://slidetodoc.com/debt-structural-adjustment-programs-saps-and-primary-health/.

[58] "The Sobering Truth About Africa's 'Resource Wealth.'" *The Afro Optimist*, theafrooptimist.com, 1 Mar. 2016, https://theafrooptimist.com/2016/03/01/the-sobering-truth-about-africas-resource-wealth/.

59 "Africa Natural Resources - Environment for Kids." *Africa Natural Resources - Environment for Kids*, sites.google. com, https://sites.google.com/site/environmentforkids/africa-natural-resources.

60 www.imf.org, https://www.imf.org/external/datamapper/NGDPD@WEO/OEMDC/ADVEC/WEOWORLD.

Manufactured by Amazon.ca
Bolton, ON